W9-AGZ-708

THE BRITANNICA GUIDE TO
THE VISUAL AND PERFORMING ARTS

THE HISTORY OF FILM

EDITED BY
NICHOLAS CROCE

Britannica Educational Publishing
IN ASSOCIATION WITH
ROSEN
EDUCATIONAL SERVICES

Published in 2016 by Britannica Educational Publishing (a trademark of Encyclopædia Britannica, Inc.) in association with The Rosen Publishing Group, Inc.
29 East 21st Street, New York, NY 10010

Distributed exclusively by Rosen Publishing.
To see additional Britannica Educational Publishing titles, go to rosenpublishing.com.

First Edition

Britannica Educational Publishing
J. E. Luebering: Director, Core Reference Group
Anthony L. Green: Editor, Compton's by Britannica

Rosen Publishing
Hope Lourie Killcoyne: Executive Editor
Nicholas Croce: Editor
Nelson Sá: Art Director
Michael Moy: Designer
Cindy Reiman: Photography Manager

Library of Congress Cataloging-in-Publication Data

The history of film/edited by Nicholas Croce.
pages cm.—(The Britannica guide to the visual and performing arts)
Includes bibliographical references and index.
ISBN 978-1-68048-076-4 (library bound)
1. Motion pictures—History—Juvenile literature. I. Croce, Nicholas, editor.
PN1993.5.A1H5475 2015
791.4309—dc23

2014039601

Manufactured in the United States of America

Photo credits: Cover, p. i Steve Sands/GC Images/Getty Images; p. vii © iStockphoto.com/danr13; p. viii © iStockphoto.com/iofoto; p. xi © iStockphoto.com/RobertCravens; pp. 2–3 Courtesy of the British Film Institute, London; pp. 9, 176–177, 183 Courtesy Everett Collection; p. 15 Photofest; p. 24 Mary Evans/Ronald Grant/Everett Collection; p. 35 Courtesy of the Museum of Modern Art/Film Stills Archive, NY; pp. 38–39, 69 From a private collection; p. 53 Goskino/photograph, the Museum of Modern Art/Film Stills Archive, NY; pp. 62–63 © 1931 United Artists Corporation, photograph from a private collection; pp. 78–79 Silver Screen Collection/Moviepix/Getty Images; pp. 86–87 Copyright © 1939 Metro-Goldwyn-Mayer Inc.; pp. 96–97 © 1940 Twentieth Century-Fox Film Corporation, photograph from a private collection; pp. 98–99 Copyright © 1941 RKO Pictures, a division of RKO General; p. 111 Copyright © 1941 Paramount Pictures; p. 115 © 1963 Embassy Pictures Corporation, photograph from a private collection; p. 124 Leacock Pennebaker, Inc., photograph from a private collection; p. 130 Courtesy of United Artists Corporation; p. 131 Copyright © 1968 Metro-Goldwyn-Mayer Inc; p. 139 © Toho Company/Courtesy Everett Collection; p. 144 © Sony Pictures Entertainment Inc., photo, Chan Kam Chuen; p. 153 Sigma III/Filmove Studio Barrandov; pp. 162–163 © 1969 Columbia Pictures Corporation, photograph from a private collection; pp. 166–167 © 1976 United Artists Corporation, photograph from a private collection; p. 185 Copyright © 2005 Universal Pictures and Wing Nut Films; p. 193 © 2006 Miramax Films, all rights reserved; p. 195 Copyright © 1992 Warner Brothers, Inc.; cover and interior pages graphic elements David M. Schrader/Shutterstock.com, E_K/Shutterstock.com, Valentin Agapov/Shutterstock.com, argus/Shutterstock.com, Iakov Filimonov/Shutterstock.com.

CONTENTS

CHAPTER 4

CHAPTER 5

The viewing of motion pictures, or film, began as an experience limited to a one-person audience. Soon after, the advent of motion-picture projection transformed the medium predominantly into a form of theatrical entertainment viewed by large numbers of people simultaneously. By the end of the 20th century, new technologies had made possible a wide variety of viewing options, ranging from the solitary spectator to audiences of thousands in a single space or of millions over many venues.

The Kinetoscope, the first motion-picture viewing device, was invented by Thomas Alva Edison and William Dickson in 1891. It allowed only a single spectator at a time to look through a peephole at the tiny moving images inside the machine. Within several years, projectors capable of enlarging the image on a screen in a theatrical space had been developed. Projected motion pictures soon rendered the

In the 20th century, watching movies became an experience that people wanted to share with others.

peephole viewers obsolete, although the latter could still be found for decades as novelties in penny arcades and amusement parks.

The motion picture thrived in the first half of the 20th century as a mass medium centred on theatrical exhibition. Attending motion pictures became a social experience shared among friends or in an audience of strangers. Although the physical setting was similar to live events such as stage or concert performances, fundamental differences arose in the viewing of mechanically reproduced images rather than living persons. Motion-picture audiences were more informal in dress and demeanour. Eating and drinking during screenings became common; indeed, the sale of items such as popcorn and soft drinks proved more lucrative to many exhibitors than box-office admissions. Consecutive repeat showings permitted patrons to enter and leave in the middle of programs, giving rise to the expression "This is where I came in," which became obsolete and largely unknown by the end of the 20th century, when theatres were cleared after each screening.

During the second half of the 20th century, television became a popular medium for watching movies.

When television emerged as a competing home-entertainment medium after World War II, theatrical motion-picture attendance suffered a severe decline. However, older motion pictures became a staple of television programming, and television in turn began to serve as a significant advertising medium for promoting new films. While the television presentation of motion pictures varied in different countries, in the United States it was common on commercial broadcast channels to divide up the screening with frequent commercial breaks. After the introduction in the mid-1950s of CinemaScope and other widescreen formats for motion pictures in theatrical release—a technological innovation intended to highlight the value of the large-screen theatre experience in contrast to the then small-screen home medium—these works were later altered for television release. In a technique called "panning and scanning," the original versions of widescreen films were rephotographed, sometimes with new camera movements added, to record significant screen events for the narrower television frame.

In the later decades of the 20th century, as theatrical motion-picture attendance stabilized at much lower numbers than before World War II, the television became the predominant exhibition venue for motion pictures. In the 1980s the home-viewing experience dramatically expanded with the emergence of cable television, with channels playing up-to-date motion pictures without commercial breaks, and especially with the development of the videocassette recorder (VCR), a device that could record television signals on cassettes of magnetic tape as well as play prerecorded cassettes. Motion-picture companies released recent and older films in videocassette format, and neighbourhood video stores sprang up to rent or sell cassettes. Home viewers could choose what they wanted to see and take home motion pictures on video in much the same way as they might select a book to read or recorded music to listen to.

Newer technologies introduced at the end of the 20th and the beginning of the 21st centuries broadened the home viewing of motion pictures still further. Systems delivering television signals via satellite or digital cable offered hundreds of channels, many of them playing motion pictures continuously. The 1990s witnessed the introduction of the DVD (digital video disc, or digital versatile disc), which converts analog audio and video signals into binary data that can then be read by a low-power laser. The DVD was a medium for recording, storing, and playing motion pictures that provided significantly more space for data than the videotape cassette—so much more, in fact, that even early DVDs contained motion pictures in both their original widescreen theatrical-release format (i.e., in "letterboxed" form, a term referring to the black bands that appear above and below the image on a television with a roughly square aspect ratio of 4 to 3) and in the "panned and scanned" version. Sound tracks were made available

By the end of the 20th and the beginning of the 21st centuries, DVDs became the primary technology used to distribute film.

in original or dubbed languages, and a variety of supplemental materials included voice-over commentaries from directors and other creative personnel, documentaries on the making of the film, preview trailers, screen tests, and more. The Blu-ray format, adopted as an industry standard in 2008, promised optical discs with even greater data capacity. The first decade of the 21st century also brought the widespread adoption of video-on-demand (VOD), in which home viewers could request instant delivery of motion pictures of their choice directly to their television or computer screens. Internet-based VOD played an increasing role in the distribution and circulation of motion pictures, as did P2P (peer-to-peer) file sharing, the latter of which was seen as a threat by motion-picture studios. While theatrical exhibition continued to play a significant role and theatres retained their value as social gathering places that could present large-scale images, the dominant trend in the experience of motion pictures gave home viewers increasing control over what films to see, when to see them, and how to see them. Viewers were able to stop the image, enlarge it, reverse it, fast forward, skip to desired scenes, and take charge as never before over the process of screening itself.

Within the first two decades of motion pictures, a wide range of discussion about the medium had developed, at many levels of appreciation and analysis—newspaper reviews, professional trade periodicals, books on production technique, fan magazines, and gossip columns, among others. By the World War I era there were even scholarly monographs and the first university courses. In the 1930s archives were founded on the model of, and sometimes associated with, art museums, to collect films for posterity and make important works available for public appreciation. As new media have emerged, sometimes rivaling motion pictures in popularity, they have nevertheless offered additional venues for commentary on many aspects of film.

At the beginning of the 21st century, for example, the Internet provided uncounted thousands of Web sites for information and opinions on motion pictures, stars, directors, the industry, film history, and much more. Both broadcast and cable television channels offered regular programming and frequent specials with news on the lives of actors and the making of new films. Some magazines were devoted entirely to covering the entertainment media, while nearly every popular periodical and newspaper gave coverage to motion-picture personalities, new films, and industry developments. Interest in major Hollywood blockbusters extended to the reporting of how these mega-releases fared each weekend at the box office, with films ranked by income as if they were competing in a sporting event. (Some of this coverage could be explained as a promotional effort by media conglomerates that operate movie studios along with newspapers, television stations, and Internet sites.)

Film studies in universities and colleges greatly expanded beginning in the 1970s, an expansion based in part on a growing recognition that the medium's artistic achievements were worthy of study and also on the view that its cultural influence in conveying political and social attitudes to wide audiences required analysis and critique. Teaching and scholarship—assisted by the growing availability of older works through archives, television and cable programming, and video and DVD release—explored social issues such as how race, class, and gender were represented in films. Motion-picture genres, directors and stars, industrial practices, and national cinemas became subjects for courses of study and research. University presses annually published dozens of scholarly books on film history, theory, and aesthetics, as well as sponsoring or distributing academic journals.

The permanence of the motion-picture medium—the fact that film can be stored and reproduced indefinitely—makes it not only an enduring theatrical art but also a vivid record of past life. Despite the fact that motion pictures can theoretically last forever, relatively few have been preserved, and many of these are in poor condition. One reason is that inflammable nitrate film stock, which was generally used until the 1940s, when it was replaced by acetate, is chemically unstable. Also, as film runs through a projector, it is eventually worn, scratched, or damaged. Still another factor is that commercial conditions of filmmaking discouraged preservation;

the stress was on the present and the future, not on preservation of the past. Early motion pictures were best preserved when filmmakers such as Charlie Chaplin and Walt Disney had control over their own work and a personal interest in preserving and representing it. During the 1960s and '70s, however, there developed a tremendous interest in old movies. Revival houses sprang up in most major American cities, and distribution companies were established solely for the reissue of old films.

Film preservation that allows access to old motion pictures is costly, requiring careful scientific control of storage conditions. The earliest film archive was the Swedish Film History Collection begun in 1933. Archives in Paris, London, and New York City followed shortly afterward. An international federation (FIAF; Fédération Internationale des Archives du Film), with headquarters in Paris, was founded in 1938.

Archivists of film face many problems: first, selecting the motion pictures to be preserved; second, acquiring copies (a negative or a fine-grain positive if possible) in good condition; third, storing them under the best-possible conditions of temperature and humidity; fourth, cataloging them and keeping some record of their contents; and fifth, allowing them to be viewed or letting stills or extracts be taken without damaging the copies. The ideal solution to the problem of choice would be to preserve everything, but the cost would be prohibitive. Even with a limited selection, acquisition and storage are expensive and difficult, and nitrate film requires regular testing to determine whether it has deteriorated enough to require copying.

The preservation of colour films has presented perhaps the most serious difficulties. While Technicolor films (mostly made before 1953) can be reproduced faithfully and endlessly, virtually all colour films made since 1953 are subject to fading that can be arrested only by storing prints at very low temperatures. Video technology has been used to help preserve some colour motion pictures; computer-driven viewers are able to read the original tints of films and reproduce them on videotape. Nevertheless, until the development of a suitable and inexpensive base onto which colour films can be transferred, the majority of colour motion pictures made after 1953 will continue to deteriorate. This volume offers a history of motion pictures and how, from economic, political, and artistic perspectives, the medium has evolved over the last century.

CHAPTER ONE

ORIGINS: EARLY YEARS, 1830–1910

The illusion of motion pictures is based on the optical phenomena known as persistence of vision and the phi phenomenon. The first of these causes the brain to retain images cast upon the retina of the eye for a fraction of a second beyond their disappearance from the field of sight, while the latter creates apparent movement between images when they succeed one another rapidly. Together these phenomena permit the succession of still frames on a motion-picture film strip to represent continuous movement when projected at the proper speed (traditionally 16 frames per second for silent films and 24 frames per second for sound films). Before the invention of photography, a variety of optical toys exploited this effect by mounting successive phase drawings of things in motion on the face of a twirling disk (the phenakistoscope, c. 1832) or inside a rotating drum (the zoetrope, c. 1834). Then, in 1839, Louis-Jacques-Mandé Daguerre, a French painter,

A series of photographs taken in 1887 by Eadweard Muybridge of a running horse.

perfected the positive photographic process known as the daguerreotype, and that same year the English scientist William Henry Fox Talbot successfully demonstrated a negative photographic process that theoretically allowed unlimited positive prints to be produced from each negative. As photography was innovated and refined over the next few decades, it became possible to replace the phase drawings in the early optical toys and devices with individually posed phase photographs, a practice that was widely and popularly carried out.

There would be no true motion pictures, however, until live action could be photographed spontaneously and simultaneously. This required a reduction in exposure time from the hour or so necessary for the pioneer photographic processes to the one-hundredth (and, ultimately, one-thousandth) of a second achieved in 1870. It also required the development of the technology of series photography by the British American photographer Eadweard Muybridge between 1872 and 1877. During that time, Muybridge was employed by Governor Leland Stanford of California, a zealous racehorse breeder, to prove that at some point in its gallop a running horse lifts all four hooves off the ground at once. Conventions of 19th-century illustration suggested otherwise, and the movement itself occurred too rapidly for perception by the naked eye, so Muybridge experimented with multiple cameras to take successive photographs of horses in motion. Finally, in 1877, he set up a battery of 12 cameras along a Sacramento racecourse with wires stretched across the track to operate their shutters. As a horse strode down the track, its hooves tripped each shutter individually to expose a successive photograph of the gallop, confirming Stanford's belief. When Muybridge later mounted these images on a rotating disk and projected them on a screen through a magic lantern, they produced a "moving picture" of the horse at full gallop as it had actually occurred in life.

The French physiologist Étienne-Jules Marey took the first series photographs with a single instrument in 1882; once again the impetus was the analysis of motion too rapid for perception by the human eye. Marey invented the chronophotographic gun, a camera shaped like a rifle that recorded 12 successive photographs per second, in order to study the movement of birds in flight. These images were imprinted on a rotating glass plate (later, paper roll film), and Marey subsequently attempted to project them. Like Muybridge, however, Marey was interested in deconstructing movement rather than synthesizing it, and he did not carry his experiments much beyond the realm of high-speed, or instantaneous, series photography. Muybridge and Marey, in fact, conducted their work in the spirit of scientific inquiry; they both extended and elaborated existing technologies in order to probe and analyze events that occurred beyond the threshold of human perception. Those who came after would return their discoveries to the realm of normal human vision and exploit them for profit.

In 1887 in Newark, New Jersey, an Episcopalian minister named Hannibal Goodwin developed the idea of using celluloid as a base for photographic emulsions. The inventor and industrialist George Eastman, who had earlier experimented with sensitized paper rolls for still photography, began manufacturing celluloid roll film in 1889 at his plant in Rochester, New York. This event was crucial to the development of cinematography: series photography such as Marey's chronophotography could employ glass plates or paper strip film because it recorded events of short duration in a relatively small number of images, but cinematography would inevitably find its subjects in longer, more complicated events, requiring thousands of images and therefore just the kind of flexible but durable recording medium represented by celluloid. It remained for someone to combine the principles embodied in the apparatuses of Muybridge and Marey with celluloid strip film to arrive at a viable motion-picture camera—an innovation achieved by William Kennedy Laurie Dickson in the West Orange, New Jersey, laboratories of the Edison Company.

MÉLIÈS AND PORTER

The shift in consciousness away from films as animated photographs to films as stories, or narratives, began to take place about the turn of the 20th century and is most evident in the work of the French filmmaker Georges Méliès. Méliès was a professional magician who had become interested in the illusionist possibilities of the cinématographe—the camera-projector recently invented by the Lumière brothers. When the Lumière brothers refused to sell him one, he bought an animatograph projector from scientific-instrument maker Robert W. Paul in 1896 and reversed its mechanical principles to design his own camera. The following year he organized the Star Film company and constructed a small glass-enclosed studio on

EDISON AND THE LUMIÈRE BROTHERS

Thomas Alva Edison invented the phonograph in 1877, and it quickly became the most popular home-entertainment device of the century. It was to provide a visual accompaniment to the phonograph that Edison commissioned William Kennedy Laurie Dickson, a young laboratory assistant, to invent a motion-picture camera in 1888. Dickson built upon the work of Muybridge and Marey, a fact that he readily acknowledged, but he was the first to combine the two final essentials of motion-picture recording and viewing technology. These were a device, adapted from the escapement mechanism of a clock, to ensure the intermittent but regular motion of the film strip through the camera and a regularly perforated celluloid film strip to ensure precise synchronization between the film strip and the shutter. Dickson's camera, the Kinetograph, initially imprinted up to 50 feet (15 metres) of celluloid film at the rate of about 40 frames per second.

Because Edison had originally conceived of motion pictures as an adjunct to his phonograph, he did not commission the

(continued on the next page)

(*continued from the previous page*)

invention of a projector to accompany the Kinetograph. Rather, he had Dickson design a type of peep-show viewing device called the Kinetoscope, in which a continuous 47-foot (14-metre) film loop ran on spools between an incandescent lamp and a shutter for individual viewing. Starting in 1894, Kinetoscopes were marketed commercially through the firm of Raff and Gammon for $250 to $300 apiece. The Edison Company established its own Kinetograph studio (a single-room building called the "Black Maria" that rotated on tracks to follow the sun) in West Orange, New Jersey, to supply films for the Kinetoscopes that Raff and Gammon were installing in penny arcades, hotel lobbies, amusement parks, and other such semipublic places. In April of that year the first Kinetoscope parlour was opened in a converted storefront in New York City. The parlour charged 25 cents for admission to a bank of five machines.

The syndicate of Maguire and Baucus acquired the foreign rights to the Kinetoscope in 1894 and began to market the machines. Edison opted not to file for international patents on either his camera or his viewing device, and, as a result, the machines were

Thomas Edison's Kinetoscope record of a sneeze (also known as Fred Ott's sneeze), by W.K.L. Dickson, Orange, N.J., Jan. 9, 1894.

widely and legally copied throughout Europe, where they were modified and improved far beyond the American originals. In fact, it was a Kinetoscope exhibition in Paris that inspired the Lumière brothers, Auguste and Louis, to invent the first commercially viable projector. Their cinématographe, which functioned as a camera and printer as well as a projector, ran at the economical speed of 16 frames per second. It was given its first commercial demonstration on December 28, 1895.

Unlike the Kinetograph, which was battery-driven and weighed more than 1,000 pounds (453 kg), the cinématographe was hand-cranked, lightweight (less than 20 pounds [9

(continued on the next page)

(*continued from the previous page*)

kg]), and relatively portable. This naturally affected the kinds of films that were made with each machine: Edison films initially featured material such as circus or vaudeville acts that could be taken into a small studio to perform before an inert camera, while early Lumière films were mainly documentary views, or "actualities," shot outdoors on location. In both cases, however, the films themselves were composed of a single unedited shot emphasizing lifelike movement; they contained little or no narrative content. (After a few years design changes in the machines made it possible for Edison and the Lumières to shoot the same kinds of subjects.) In general, Lumière technology became the European standard during the early primitive era, and, because the Lumières sent their cameramen all over the world in search of exotic subjects, the cinématographe became the founding instrument of distant cinemas in Russia, Australia, and Japan.

the grounds of his house at Montreuil, where he produced, directed, photographed, and acted in more than 500 films between 1896 and 1913.

Initially Méliès used stop-motion photography (the camera and action are stopped while something is added to or removed from the scene; then filming and action are continued) to make one-shot "trick" films in which objects disappeared and reappeared or transformed themselves into other objects entirely. These films were widely imitated by producers in England and the United States. Soon, however, Méliès began to experiment with brief multiscene films, such as *L'Affaire Dreyfus* (*The Dreyfus Affair*, 1899), his first, which followed the logic of linear temporality to establish causal sequences and tell simple stories. By 1902 he had produced the influential 30-scene narrative *Le Voyage dans la lune* (*A Trip to the Moon*). Adapted from a novel by Jules Verne, it was nearly one reel in length (about 825 feet [251 metres], or 14 minutes).

The first film to achieve international distribution (mainly through piracy), *Le Voyage dans la lune* was an enormous popular success. It helped to make Star Film one of the world's largest producers (an American branch was opened in 1903) and to establish the fiction film as the cinema's mainstream product. In both respects Méliès dethroned the Lumières' cinema of actuality, films shot outdoors or on location, not on a stage set. Despite his innovations, Méliès's productions remained essentially filmed stage plays. He conceived them quite literally as successions of living pictures or, as he termed them, "artificially arranged scenes." From his earliest trick films through his last successful fantasy, *La Conquête du pole* ("The Conquest of the Pole," 1912), Méliès treated the frame of the film as the proscenium arch of a theatre stage, never once moving his camera or changing its position within a scene. He ultimately lost his audience in the late 1910s to filmmakers with more sophisticated narrative techniques.

The origination of many such techniques is closely associated with the work of Edwin S. Porter, a freelance projectionist and engineer who joined the Edison Company in 1900 as production head of its new skylight studio on East 21st Street in New York City. For the next few years, he served as director-cameraman for much of Edison's output, starting with simple one-shot films (*Kansas Saloon Smashers*, 1901) and progressing rapidly to trick films (*The Finish of Bridget McKeen*, 1901) and short multiscene narratives based on political cartoons and contemporary events (*Sampson-Schley Controversy*, 1901; *Execution of Czolgosz, with Panorama of Auburn Prison*, 1901). Porter also filmed the extraordinary *Pan-American Exposition by Night* (1901), which used time-lapse photography to produce a circular panorama of the exposition's electrical illumination, and the 10-scene *Jack and the Beanstalk* (1902), a narrative that simulates the sequencing of lantern slides to achieve a logical, if elliptical, spatial continuity.

It was probably Porter's experience as a projectionist at the Eden Musée theatre in 1898 that ultimately led him in the early 1900s to the practice of continuity editing. The process of selecting one-shot films and arranging them into a 15-minute program for screen presentation was very much like that of constructing a single film out of a series of separate shots. Porter, by his own admission, was also influenced by other filmmakers—especially Méliès, whose *Le Voyage dans la lune* he came to know well in the process of duplicating it for illegal distribution by Edison in October 1902. Years later Porter claimed that the Méliès film had given him the notion of "telling a story in continuity form," which resulted in *The Life of an American Fireman* (about 400 feet [122 metres], or six minutes, produced in late 1902 and released in January 1903). This film, which was also influenced by James Williamson's *Fire!,* combined archival footage with staged scenes to create a nine-shot narrative of a dramatic rescue from a burning building. It was for years the subject of controversy because in a later version the last two scenes were intercut, or crosscut, into a 14-shot parallel sequence. It is now generally believed that in the earliest version of the film these scenes, which repeat the same rescue operation from an interior and exterior point of view, were shown in their entirety, one after the other. This repetition, or overlapping continuity, which owes much to magic lantern shows, clearly defines the spatial relationships between scenes but leaves temporal relationships underdeveloped and, to modern sensibilities, confused. Contemporary audiences, however, were conditioned by lantern slide projections and even comic strips; they understood a sequence of motion-picture shots to be a series of individual moving photographs, each of which was self-contained within its frame. Spatial relationships were clear in such earlier narrative forms because their only medium was space.

Motion pictures, however, exist in time as well as space, and the major problem for early filmmakers was the establishment of temporal continuity from one shot to the next. Porter's *The Great Train Robbery* (1903) is widely acknowledged to be the first narrative film to have achieved such continuity of action. Comprising 14 separate shots of noncontinuous, nonoverlapping action, the film contains an early example of parallel editing, two credible back, or rear, projections (the projection from the rear of previously filmed action or scenery onto a translucent screen to provide the background for new action filmed in front of the screen), two camera pans, and several shots composed diagonally and staged in depth—a major departure from the frontally composed, theatrical staging of Méliès.

The industry's first spectacular box-office success, *The Great Train Robbery* is credited with establishing the realistic narrative, as opposed to Méliès-style fantasy, as the commercial cinema's dominant form. The film's popularity encouraged investors and led to the establishment of the first

Still from Edwin S. Porter's *The Great Train Robbery* (1903).

permanent film theatres, or nickelodeons, across the country. Running about 12 minutes, it also helped to boost standard film length toward one reel, or 1,000 feet (305 metres [about 16 minutes at the average silent speed]). Despite the film's success, Porter continued to practice overlapping action in such conventional narratives as *Uncle Tom's Cabin* (1903) and the social justice dramas *The Ex-Convict* (1904) and *The Kleptomaniac* (1905). He experimented with model animation in *The Dream of a Rarebit Fiend* (1906) and *The Teddy Bears* (1907) but lost interest in the creative aspects of filmmaking as the process became increasingly industrialized. He left Edison in 1909 to pursue a career as a producer and equipment manufacturer. Porter, like Méliès, could not adapt to the linear narrative modes and assembly-line production systems that were developing.

EARLY GROWTH OF THE FILM INDUSTRY

Méliès's decline was assisted by the industrialization of the French and, for a time, the entire European cinema by the Pathé Frères company, founded in 1896 by the former phonograph importer Charles Pathé. Financed by some of France's largest corporations, Pathé acquired the Lumière patents in 1902 and commissioned the design of an improved studio camera that soon dominated the market on both sides of the Atlantic (it has been estimated that, before 1918, 60 percent of all films were shot with a Pathé camera). Pathé also manufactured his own film stock and in 1902 established a vast production facility at Vincennes where films were turned out on an assembly-line basis under the managing direction of Ferdinand Zecca. The following year, Pathé began to open foreign sales agencies, which would soon become full-blown production companies—Hispano Film (1906), Pathé-Rouss, Moscow (1907), Film d'Arte Italiano (1909), Pathé-Britannia, London (1909), and Pathé-America (1910). He acquired permanent exhibition sites, building the world's first luxury cinema (the Omnia-Pathé) in Paris in 1906. In 1911 Pathé became Méliès's distributor and helped to drive Star Film out of business.

Pathé's only serious rival on the Continent at this time was Gaumont Pictures, founded by the engineer-inventor Léon Gaumont in 1895. Though never more than one-fourth the size of Pathé, Gaumont followed the same pattern of expansion, manufacturing its own equipment and mass-producing films under a supervising director (through 1906, Alice Guy, the cinema's first female director; afterward, Louis Feuillade). Like Pathé, Gaumont opened foreign offices and acquired theatre chains. From 1905 to 1914 its studios at La Villette, France, were the largest in the world. Pathé and Gaumont dominated pre-World War I motion-picture production, exhibition, and sales in Europe, and they effectively brought to an end the artisanal mode of filmmaking practiced by Méliès and his British contemporaries.

In the United States a similar pattern was emerging through the formation of film exchanges and the consolidation of an industrywide monopoly based on the pooling of patent rights. About 1897 producers had adopted the practice of selling prints outright, which had the effect of promoting itinerant exhibition and discriminating against the owners of permanent sites. In 1903, in response to the needs of theatre owners, Harry J. Miles and Herbert Miles opened a film exchange in San Francisco. The exchange functioned as a broker between producers and exhibitors, buying prints from the former and leasing them to the latter for 25 percent of the purchase price (in subsequent practice, rental fees were calculated on individual production costs and box-office receipts). The exchange system of distribution quickly caught on because it profited nearly everyone: the new middlemen made fortunes by collecting multiple revenues on the same prints; exhibitors were able to reduce their overheads and vary their programs without financial risk; and, ultimately, producers experienced a tremendous surge in demand for their product as exhibition and distribution boomed nationwide. (Between November 1906 and March 1907, for example, producers increased their weekly output from 10,000 to 28,000 feet [3,000 to 8,500 metres] and still could not meet demand.)

The most immediate effect of the rapid rise of the distribution sector was the nickelodeon boom, the exponential growth of permanent film theatres in the United States from a mere handful in 1904 to between 8,000 and 10,000 by 1908. Named for the Nickelodeon (ersatz Greek for "nickel theatre"), which opened in Pittsburgh in 1905, these theatres were makeshift facilities lodged in converted storefronts. They showed approximately an hour's worth of films for an admission price of 5 to 10 cents. Originally identified with working-class audiences, nickelodeons appealed increasingly to the middle class as the decade wore on, and they became associated with the rising popularity of the story film. Their spread also forced the standardization of film length at one reel, or 1,000 feet (305 metres), to facilitate high-efficiency production and the trading of products within the industry.

By 1908 there were about 20 motion-picture production companies operating in the United States. They were constantly at war with one another over business practices and patent rights, and they had begun to fear that their fragmentation would cause them to lose control of the industry to the two new sectors of distribution and exhibition. The most powerful among them—Edison, Biograph, Vitagraph, Essanay, Kalem, Selig Polyscope, Lubin, the American branches of the French Star Film and Pathé Frères, and Kleine Optical, the largest domestic distributor of foreign films—therefore entered into a collusive trade agreement to ensure their continued dominance. On September 9, 1908, these companies formed the Motion Picture Patents Company (MPPC), pooling the 16 most significant U.S. patents for motion-picture technology and entering into an exclusive contract with the Eastman Kodak Company for the supply of raw film stock.

The MPPC, also known as the "Trust," sought to control every segment of the industry and therefore set up a licensing system for assessing royalties. The use of its patents was granted only to licensed equipment manufacturers; film stock could be sold only to licensed producers; licensed producers and importers were required to fix rental prices at a minimum level and to set quotas for foreign footage to reduce competition; MPPC films could be sold only to licensed distributors, who could lease them only to licensed exhibitors; and only licensed exhibitors had the right to use MPPC projectors and rent company films. To solidify its control, in 1910—the same year in which motion-picture attendance in the United States rose to 26 million persons a week—the MPPC formed the General Film Company, which integrated the licensed distributors into a single corporate entity. Although it was clearly monopolistic in practice and intent, the MPPC helped to stabilize the American film industry during a period of unprecedented growth and change by standardizing exhibition practice, increasing the efficiency of distribution, and regularizing pricing in all three sectors. Its collusive nature, however, provoked a reaction that ultimately destroyed it.

In a sense, the MPPC's ironclad efforts to eliminate competition merely fostered it. Almost from the outset there was widespread resistance to the MPPC on the part of independent distributors (numbering 10 or more in early 1909) and exhibitors (estimated at 2,000 to 2,500), and in January 1909 they formed their own trade association, the Independent Film Protective Association—reorganized that fall as the National Independent Moving Picture Alliance—to provide financial and legal support against the Trust. A more effective and powerful anti-Trust organization was the Motion Picture Distributing and Sales Company, which began operation in May 1910 (three weeks after the inception of General Film) and which eventually came to serve 47 exchanges in 27 cities. For nearly two years, independents were able to present a united front through the company, which finally split into two rival camps in the spring of 1912 (the Mutual Film Corporation and the Universal Film Manufacturing Company).

By imitating MPPC practices of joining forces and licensing, the early independents were able to compete effectively against the Trust in its first three years of operation, netting about 40 percent of all American film business. In fact, their product, the one-reel short, and their mode of operation were initially fundamentally the same as the MPPC's. The independents later revolutionized the industry, however, by adopting the multiple-reel film as their basic product, a move that caused the MPPC to embrace the one-reeler with a vengeance, hastening its own demise.

CHAPTER TWO

THE SILENT YEARS, 1910–27

Multiple-reel films had appeared in the United States as early as 1907, when Adolph Zukor distributed Pathé's three-reel *Passion Play*, but when Vitagraph produced the five-reel *The Life of Moses* in 1909, the MPPC forced it to be released in serial fashion at the rate of one reel a week. The multiple-reel film—which came to be called a "feature," in the vaudevillian sense of a headline attraction—achieved general acceptance with the smashing success of Louis Mercanton's three-and-one-half-reel *La Reine Elisabeth* (*Queen Elizabeth*, 1912), which starred Sarah Bernhardt and was imported by Zukor (who founded the independent Famous Players production company with its profits). In 1912 Enrico Guazzoni's nine-reel Italian superspectacle *Quo Vadis?* ("Whither Are You Going?") was road-shown in legitimate theatres across the country at a top admission price of one dollar, and the feature craze was on.

French actress Sarah Bernhardt (1844-1923).

At first there were difficulties in distributing features, because the exchanges associated with both the MPPC and the independents were geared toward cheaply made one-reel shorts. Because of their more elaborate production values, features had relatively higher negative costs. This was a disadvantage to distributors, who charged a uniform price per foot. By 1914, however, several national feature-distribution alliances that correlated pricing with a film's negative cost and box-office receipts were organized. These new exchanges demonstrated the economic advantage of multiple-reel films over shorts. Exhibitors quickly learned that features could command higher admission prices and longer runs; single-title packages were also cheaper and easier to advertise than programs of multiple titles. As for manufacturing, producers found that the higher expenditure for features was readily amortized by high volume sales to distributors, who in turn were eager to share in the higher admission returns from the theatres. The whole industry soon reorganized itself around the economics of the multiple-reel film, and the effects of this restructuring did much to give motion pictures their characteristic modern form.

Feature films made motion pictures respectable for the middle class by providing a format that was analogous to that of the legitimate theatre and was suitable for the adaptation of middle-class novels and plays. This new audience had more demanding standards than the older working-class one, and producers readily increased their budgets to provide high technical quality and elaborate productions. The new viewers also had a more refined sense of comfort, which exhibitors quickly accommodated by replacing their storefronts with large, elegantly appointed new theatres in the major urban centres (one of the first was Mitchell L. Marks's 3,300-seat Strand, which opened in the Broadway district of Manhattan in 1914). Known as "dream palaces" because of the fantastic luxuriance of their interiors, these houses had to show features rather than a program of shorts to attract large audiences at premium prices. By 1916 there were more than 21,000 movie theatres in the United States. Their advent marked the end of the nickelodeon era and foretold the rise of the Hollywood studio system, which dominated urban exhibition from the 1920s to the '50s. Before the new studio-based monopoly could be established, however, the patents-based monopoly of the MPPC had to expire, and this it did about 1914 as a result of its own basic assumptions.

As conceived by Edison, the basic operating principle of the Trust was to control the industry through patents pooling and licensing, an idea logical enough in theory but difficult to practice in the context of a dynamically changing marketplace.

Specifically, the Trust's failure to anticipate the independents' widespread and aggressive resistance to its policies cost it a fortune in patent-infringement litigation. Furthermore, the Trust badly underestimated the importance of the feature film, permitting the independents to claim this popular new product as entirely their own. Another issue that the MPPC misjudged was the power of the marketing strategy known as the "star system." Borrowed from the theatre industry, this system involves the creation and management of publicity about key performers, or stars, to stimulate demand for their films. Trust company producers used this kind of publicity after 1910, when Carl Laemmle of Independent Motion Pictures (IMP) promoted Florence Lawrence into national stardom through a series of media stunts in St. Louis, Missouri, but they never exploited the technique as forcefully or as imaginatively as the independents did. Finally, and most decisively, in August 1912 the U.S. Justice Department brought suit against the MPPC for "restraint of trade" in violation of the Sherman Antitrust Act. Delayed by countersuits and by World War I, the government's case was eventually won, and the MPPC formally dissolved in 1918, although it had been functionally inoperative since 1914.

The rise and fall of the MPPC was concurrent with the industry's move to southern California. As a result of the nickelodeon boom, some exhibitors—who showed three separate programs over a seven-day period—had begun to require as many as 20 new films per week, and it became necessary to put production on a systematic year-round schedule. Because most films were still shot outdoors in available light, such schedules could not be maintained in the vicinity of New York City or Chicago, where the industry had originally located itself in order to take advantage of trained theatrical labour pools. As early as 1907, production companies, such as Selig Polyscope, began to dispatch production units to warmer climates during winter. It was soon clear that what producers required was a new industrial centre—one with warm weather, a temperate climate, a variety of scenery, and other qualities (such as access to acting talent) essential to their highly unconventional form of manufacturing.

Various companies experimented with location shooting in Jacksonville, Florida, in San Antonio, Texas, in Santa Fe, New Mexico, and even in Cuba, but the ultimate site of the American film industry was a Los Angeles suburb (originally a small industrial town) called Hollywood. It is generally thought that Hollywood's distance from the MPPC's headquarters in New York City made it attractive to the independents, but MPPC members such as Selig, Kalem, Biograph, and Essanay had also established facilities there by 1911 in response to a number of the region's attractions. These included the temperate climate required for year-round production (the U.S. Weather Bureau estimated that an average of 320 days per year were sunny or clear); a wide range of topography within a 50-mile (80-km) radius of Hollywood, including mountains, valleys, forests, lakes, islands, seacoast, and desert; the status of Los Angeles as a professional theatrical centre; the existence of a low tax base; and the presence of cheap and plentiful labour and land. This latter factor enabled the newly arrived production companies to buy up tens of thousands of acres of prime real estate on which to locate their studios, standing sets, and backlots.

By 1915 approximately 15,000 workers were employed by the motion-picture industry in Hollywood, and more than 60 percent of American production was centred there. In that same year the trade journal *Variety* reported that capital investment in American motion pictures—the business of artisanal craftsmen and fairground operators only a decade before—had exceeded $500 million. The most powerful companies in the new film capital were the independents, who were flush with cash from their conversion to feature production. These included the Famous Players–Lasky Corporation (later Paramount Pictures, c. 1927), which was formed by a merger of Zukor's Famous Players Company, Jesse L. Lasky's Feature Play Company, and the Paramount distribution exchange in 1916; Universal Pictures, founded by Carl Laemmle in 1912 by merging IMP with Powers, Rex, Nestor, Champion, and Bison; Goldwyn Picture Corporation, founded in 1916 by Samuel Goldfish (later Goldwyn) and Edgar Selwyn; Metro Picture Corporation and Louis B. Mayer Pictures, founded by Louis B. Mayer in 1915 and 1917, respectively; and the Fox Film Corporation (later Twentieth Century–Fox, 1935), founded by William Fox in 1915. After World War I these companies were joined by Loew's, Inc. (parent corporation of MGM, created by the merger of Metro, Goldwyn, and Mayer companies cited above, 1924), a national exhibition chain organized by Marcus Loew and Nicholas Schenck in 1919; First National Pictures, Inc., a circuit of independent exhibitors who established their own production facilities in Burbank, California, in 1922; Warner Brothers Pictures, Inc., founded by Harry, Albert, Samuel, and Jack Warner in 1923; and Columbia Pictures, Inc., incorporated in 1924 by Harry Cohn and Jack Cohn.

These organizations became the backbone of the Hollywood studio system, and the men who controlled them shared several important traits. They were all independent exhibitors and distributors who had outwitted the Trust and earned their success by manipulating finances in the post-nickelodeon feature boom, merging production companies, organizing national distribution networks, and ultimately acquiring vast theatre chains. They saw their business as basically a retailing operation modeled on the practice of chain stores such as Woolworth's and Sears. Not incidentally, these men were all first- or second-generation Jewish immigrants from eastern Europe, most of them with little formal education, while the audience they served was 90 percent Protestant and Catholic. This circumstance would become an issue during the 1920s, when the movies became a mass medium that was part of the life of every U.S. citizen and when Hollywood became the chief purveyor of American culture to the world.

PRE-WORLD WAR I EUROPEAN CINEMA

Before World War I, European cinema was dominated by France and Italy. At Pathé Frères, director general Ferdinand Zecca perfected the course comique, a uniquely Gallic version of the chase film, which inspired Mack Sennett's Keystone Kops, while the immensely popular Max Linder created a comic persona that would deeply influence the work of Charlie Chaplin. The episodic crime film was pioneered by Victorin Jasset in the Nick Carter series, produced for the small Éclair Company, but it remained for Gaumont's Louis Feuillade to bring the genre to aesthetic perfection in the extremely successful serials *Fantômas* (1913–14), *Les Vampires* (1915–16), and *Judex* (1916).

Another influential phenomenon initiated in prewar France was the film d'art movement. It began with *L'Assassinat du duc de Guise* ("The Assassination of the Duke of Guise," 1908), directed by Charles Le Bargy and André Calmettes of the Comédie Française for the Société Film d'Art, which was formed for the express purpose of transferring prestigious stage plays starring famous performers to the screen. *L'Assassinat*'s success inspired other companies to make similar films, which came to be known as *films d'art*. These films were long on intellectual pedigree and short on narrative sophistication. The directors simply filmed theatrical productions in toto, without adaptation. Their brief popularity nevertheless created a context for the lengthy treatment of serious material in motion pictures and was directly instrumental in the rise of the feature.

No country, however, was more responsible for the popularity of the feature than Italy. The Italian cinema's lavishly produced costume spectacles brought it international prominence in the years before the war. The prototypes of the genre, by virtue of their epic material and length, were the Cines company's six-reel *Gli ultimi giorni di Pompei* (*The Last Days of Pompei*), directed by Luigi Maggi in 1908, and its 10-reel remake, directed by Ernesto Pasquali in 1913; but it was Cines's nine-reel *Quo Vadis?* ("Whither Are You Going?" 1912), with its huge three-dimensional sets re-creating ancient Rome and its 5,000 extras, that established the standard for the superspectacle and briefly conquered the world market for Italian motion pictures. Its successor, the Italia company's 12-reel *Cabiria* (1914), was even more extravagant in its historical reconstruction of the Second Punic War, from the burning of the Roman fleet at Syracuse to Hannibal crossing the Alps and the sack of Carthage. The Italian superspectacle stimulated public demand for features and influenced such important directors as Cecil B. DeMille, Ernst Lubitsch, and especially D.W. Griffith.

POST-WORLD WAR I EUROPEAN CINEMA

Prior to World War I, the American cinema had lagged behind the film industries of Europe, particularly those of France and Italy, in such matters as feature production and the establishment of permanent theatres. During the war, however, European film production virtually ceased, in part because the same chemicals used in the production of celluloid were necessary for the manufacture of gunpowder. The American

D.W. GRIFFITH

Although narrative film was and continues to be strongly influenced by a combination of economic, technological, and social factors, it also owes a great deal to the individual artists who viewed film as a medium of personal expression. Chief among these innovators was American director D.W. Griffith (1875-1948). It is true that Griffith's self-cultivated reputation as a Romantic artist—"the father of film technique," "the man who invented Hollywood," "the Shakespeare of the screen," and the like—is somewhat overblown. It is also true that by 1908 film narrative had already been systematically organized to accommodate the material conditions of production. Griffith's work nevertheless transformed that system from its primitive to its classical mode. He was the first filmmaker to realize that the motion-picture medium, properly vested with technical vitality and seriousness of theme, could exercise enormous persuasive power over an audience, or even a nation, without recourse to print or human speech.

Griffith was fundamentally a 19th-century man who became one of the 20th-century's greatest artists. Transcending personal

The temple of Babylon sequence from *Intolerance* (1916), directed by D.W. Griffith.

defects of vision, judgment, and taste, he developed the narrative language of film. Later filmmakers adapted his techniques and structures to new themes and styles, while for Griffith his innovations were inextricably linked to a social vision that became obsolete while he was still in the prime of his working life.

cinema, meanwhile, experienced a period of unprecedented prosperity and growth. By the end of the war, it exercised nearly total control of the international market: when the Treaty of Versailles was signed in 1919, 90 percent of all films screened in Europe, Africa, and Asia were American, and the figure for South America was (and remained through the 1950s) close to 100 percent. The main exception was Germany, which had been cut off from American films from 1914 until the end of the war.

GERMANY

Before World War I, the German motion-picture audience drew broadly from different social classes, and the country was among the leaders in the construction of film theatres. But German film production lagged behind that of several other European countries, and Denmark's film industry in particular played a more prominent role in German film exhibition than did many domestic companies. This dependence on imported films became a matter of concern among military leaders during the war, when a flood of effective anti-German propaganda films began to pour into Germany from the Allied countries. Therefore, on December 18, 1917, the German general Erich Ludendorff ordered the merger of the main German production, distribution, and exhibition companies into the government-subsidized conglomerate Universum Film Aktiengesellschaft (UFA). UFA's mission was to upgrade the quality of German films. The organization proved to be highly effective, and, when the war ended in Germany's defeat in November 1918, the German film industry was prepared for the first time to compete in the international marketplace. Transferred to private control, UFA became the single largest studio in Europe and produced most of the films associated with the "golden age" of German cinema during the Weimar Republic (1919–33).

UFA's first peacetime productions were elaborate costume dramas (*Kostümfilme*) in the vein of the prewar Italian superspectacles, and the master of this form was Ernst Lubitsch, who directed such lavish and successful historical pageants as *Madame Du Barry* (released in the United States as *Passion*, 1919), *Anna Boleyn* (*Deception*, 1920), and *Das Weib des Pharao* (*The Loves of Pharaoh*, 1921) before immigrating to the United States in 1922. These films earned the German cinema a foothold in the world market, but it was an Expressionist work, *Das Kabinett des Dr. Caligari* (*The Cabinet of Dr. Caligari*, 1919), that brought the industry its first great artistic acclaim. Based on a scenario by the Czech poet Hans Janowitz and the Austrian writer Carl Mayer, the film recounts a series of brutal murders that are committed in the north German town of Holstenwall by a somnambulist at

Still from Robert Wiene's classic Expressionist film *The Cabinet of Dr. Caligari* (1919).

the bidding of a demented mountebank, who believes he is the incarnation of a homicidal 18th-century hypnotist named Dr. Caligari. Erich Pommer, Caligari's producer at Decla-Bioskop (an independent production company that was to merge with UFA in 1921), added a scene to the original scenario so that the story appears to be narrated by a madman confined to an asylum of which the mountebank is director and head psychiatrist. To represent the narrator's tortured mental state, the director, Robert Wiene, hired three prominent Expressionist artists—Hermann Warm, Walter Röhrig, and Walter Reimann—to design sets that depicted exaggerated dimensions and deformed spatial relationships. To heighten this architectural stylization (and also to economize on electric power, which was rationed in postwar Germany), bizarre patterns of light and shadow were painted directly onto the scenery and even onto the characters' makeup.

In its effort to embody disturbed psychological states through decor, *Caligari* influenced enormously the UFA films that followed it and gave rise to the movement known as German Expressionism. The films of this movement were studio-made and often used distorted sets and lighting effects to create a highly subjective mood. They were primarily films of fantasy and terror that employed horrific plots to express the theme of the soul in search of itself. Most were photographed by one of the two great cinematographers of the Weimar period, Karl Freund and Fritz Arno Wagner. Representative works include F.W. Murnau's *Der Januskopf* (*Janus-Faced,* 1920), adapted from Robert Louis Stevenson's *Dr. Jekyll and Mr. Hyde;* Paul Wegener and Carl Boese's *Der Golem* (*The Golem,* 1920), adapted from a Jewish legend in which a gigantic clay statue becomes a raging monster; Arthur Robison's *Schatten* (*Warning Shadows,* 1922); Wiene's *Raskolnikow* (1923), based on Fyodor Dostoyevsky's *Crime and Punishment;* Paul Leni's *Das Wachsfigurenkabinett* (*Waxworks,* 1924); and Henrik Galeen's *Der Student von Prag* (*The Student of Prague,* 1926), which combines the Faust legend with a doppelgänger, or double, motif. In addition to winning international prestige for German films, Expressionism produced two directors who would become major figures in world cinema, Fritz Lang and F.W. Murnau.

Lang had already directed several successful serials, including *Die Spinnen* (*The Spiders*, 1919–20), when he collaborated with his future wife, the scriptwriter Thea von Harbou, to produce *Der müde Tod* ("The Weary Death"; English title: *Destiny*, 1921) for Decla-Bioskop. This episodic Romantic allegory of doomed lovers, set in several different historical periods, earned Lang acclaim for his dynamic compositions of architectural line and space. Lang's use of striking, stylized images is also demonstrated in the other films of his Expressionist period, notably the crime melodrama *Dr. Mabuse, der Spieler* (*Dr. Mabuse, the Gambler*, 1922), the Wagnerian diptych *Siegfried* (1922–24) and *Kriemhilds Rache* (*Kriemhild's Revenge*, 1922–23), and the stunningly futuristic *Metropolis* (1926), perhaps the greatest science-fiction film ever made. After directing the early sound masterpiece *M* (1931), based on child murders in Düsseldorf, Lang became increasingly estranged from German political life. He emigrated in 1933 to escape the Nazis and began a second career in the Hollywood studios the following year.

Murnau made several minor Expressionist films before directing one of the movement's classics, an (unauthorized) adaptation of Bram

Stoker's novel *Dracula* entitled *Nosferatu—eine Symphonie des Grauens* ("Nosferatu, a Symphony of Horror," 1922), but it was *Der letzte Mann* ("The Last Man"; English title: *The Last Laugh*, 1924), a film in the genre of Kammerspiel ("intimate theatre"), that made him world-famous. Scripted by Carl Mayer and produced by Erich Pommer for UFA, *Der letzte Mann* told the story of a hotel doorman who is humiliated by the loss of his job and—more important, apparently, in postwar German society—of his splendid paramilitary uniform. Murnau and Karl Freund, his cameraman, gave this simple tale a complex narrative structure through their innovative use of camera movement and subjective point-of-view shots. In one famous example, Freund strapped a lightweight camera to his chest and stumbled drunkenly around the set of a bedroom to record the inebriated porter's point of view. In the absence of modern cranes and dollies, at various points in the filming Murnau and Freund placed the camera on moving bicycles, fire engine ladders, and overhead cables in order to achieve smooth, sustained movement. The total effect was a tapestry of subjectively involving movement and intense identification with the narrative. Even more remarkably, the film conveyed its meaning without using any printed intertitles for dialogue or explanation.

Der letzte Mann was universally hailed as a masterpiece and probably had more influence on Hollywood style than any other single foreign film in history. Its "unchained camera" technique (Mayer's phrase) spawned many imitations in Germany and elsewhere, the most significant being E.A. Dupont's circus-tent melodrama *Variété* (1925). The film also brought Murnau a long-term Hollywood contract, which he began to fulfill in 1927 after completing two last "superproductions," *Tartüff* (*Tartuffe*, 1925) and *Faust* (1926), for UFA.

In 1924 the German mark was stabilized by the so-called Dawes Plan, which financed the long-term payment of Germany's war-reparations debt and curtailed all exports. This created an artificial prosperity in the economy at large, which lasted only until the stock market crash of 1929, but it was devastating to the film industry, the bulk of whose revenues came from foreign markets. Hollywood then seized the opportunity to cripple its only serious European rival, saturating Germany with American films and buying its independent theatre chains. As a result of these forays and its own internal mismanagement, UFA stood on the brink of bankruptcy by the end of 1925. It was saved by a $4 million loan offered by two major American studios, Famous Players–Lasky (later Paramount) and Metro-Goldwyn-Mayer, in exchange for collaborative rights to UFA studios, theatres, and creative personnel. This arrangement resulted in the founding of the Parufamet (Paramount-UFA-Metro) Distribution Company in early 1926 and the almost immediate emigration of UFA film artists and technicians to Hollywood, where they worked for a variety of studios. This first Germanic migration was temporary. Many of the filmmakers went back to UFA disgusted at the assembly-line character of the American studio system, but many—such as Lubitsch, Freund, and Murnau—stayed on to launch full-fledged Hollywood careers, and many more would return during the 1930s to escape the Nazi regime.

In the meantime, the new sensibility that had entered German intellectual life turned away from the morbid psychological themes of Expressionism toward an acceptance of "life as it is lived." Called *die neue Sachlichkeit* ("the new objectivity"), this spirit stemmed from the economic dislocations that beset German society in the wake of the war, particularly the impoverishment of the middle classes through raging inflation. In cinema, die neue Sachlichkeit translated into the grim social realism of the "street" films of the late 1920s, including G.W. Pabst's *Die freudlose Gasse* (*The Joyless Street*, 1925), Bruno Rahn's *Dirnentragödie* (*Tragedy of the Streets*, 1927), Joe May's *Asphalt* (1929), and Piel Jutzi's *Berlin-Alexanderplatz* (1931). Named for their prototype, Karl Grune's *Die Strasse* (*The Street*, 1923), these films focused on the disillusionment, cynicism, and ultimate resignation of ordinary German people whose lives were crippled during the postwar inflation.

The master of the form was G.W. Pabst, whose work established conventions of continuity editing that would become essential to the sound film. In such important realist films as *Die freudlose Gasse*, *Die Liebe der Jeanne Ney* (*The Love of Jeanne Ney*, 1927), *Die Büchse der Pandora* (*Pandora's Box*, 1929), and *Das Tagebuch einer Verlorenen* (*Diary of a Lost Girl*, 1929), Pabst created complex continuity sequences, using techniques that became key features of Hollywood's "invisible" editing style, such as cutting on action, cutting from a shot of a character's glance to one of what the character sees (motivated point-of-view shots), and cutting to a reverse angle shot (one in which the camera angle has changed 180 degrees; e.g., in a scene in which a man and a woman face one another in conversation, the man is seen from the woman's point of view, and then the woman is shown from the man's point of view). Pabst later became an important figure of the early sound period, contributing two significant works in his pacifist films *Westfront* 1918 (1930) and *Kameradschaft* ("Comradeship," 1931). Emigrating from Germany after the Nazis seized power in 1933, Pabst worked in France and briefly in Hollywood. He returned to Germany in 1941 and made several films for the Nazi-controlled film industry during World War II.

By March 1927, UFA was once again facing financial collapse, and it turned this time to the Prussian financier Alfred Hugenberg, a director of the powerful Krupp industrial empire and a leader of the right-wing German National Party who was sympathetic to the Nazis. Hugenberg bought out the American interests in UFA, acquiring a majority of the company's stock and directing the remainder into the hands of his political allies. As chairman of the UFA board, he quietly instituted a nationalistic production policy that gave increasing prominence to those allies and their cause and that enabled the Nazis to subvert the German film industry when Adolf Hitler came to power in 1933. German cinema then fell under the authority of Joseph Goebbels and his Ministry of Public Enlightenment and Propaganda. For the next 12 years every film made in the Third Reich had to be personally approved for release by Goebbels. Jews were officially banned from the industry, which caused a vast wave of German film artists to leave for Hollywood. Los Angeles became known as "the new Weimar," and the German cinema was emptied of the talent and brilliance that had created its golden age.

THE SOVIET UNION

During the decades of the Soviet Union's existence, the history of cinema in pre-Soviet Russia was a neglected subject, if not actively suppressed. In subsequent years, scholars have brought to light and reevaluated a small but vigorous film culture in the pre-World War I era. Some 4,000 motion-picture theatres were in operation, with the French company Pathé playing a substantial role in production and distribution. Meanwhile, Russian filmmakers such as Yevgeny Bauer had developed a sophisticated style marked by artful lighting and decor.

A minority party with approximately 200,000 members, the Bolsheviks had assumed the leadership of 160 million people who were scattered across the largest continuous landmass in the world, spoke more than 100 separate languages, and were mostly illiterate. Vladimir Ilich Lenin and other Bolshevik leaders looked on the motion-picture medium as a means of unifying the huge, disparate nation. Lenin was the first political leader of the 20th century to recognize both the importance of film as propaganda and its power to communicate quickly and effectively. He understood that audiences did not require literacy to comprehend a film's meaning and that more people could be reached through mass-distributed motion pictures than through any other medium of the time. Lenin declared: "The cinema is for us the most important of the arts," and his government gave top priority to the rapid development of the Soviet film industry, which was nationalized in August 1919 and put under the direct authority of Lenin's wife, Nadezhda Krupskaya.

There was, however, little to build upon. Most of the prerevolutionary producers had fled to Europe, wrecking their studios as they left and taking their equipment and film stock with them. A foreign blockade prevented the importation of new equipment or stock (there were no domestic facilities for manufacturing either), and massive power shortages restricted the use of what limited resources remained. The Cinema Committee was not deterred, however; its first act was to found a professional film school in Moscow to train directors, technicians, and actors for the cinema.

The Vsesoyuznyi Gosudarstvenyi Institut Kinematografii (VGIK; "All-Union State Institute of Cinematography") was the first such school in the world. Initially it trained people in the production of *agitki*, existing newsreels reedited for the purpose of agitation and propaganda (agitprop). The *agitki* were transported on specially equipped agit-trains and agit-steamers to the provinces, where they were exhibited to generate support for the Revolution. (The state-controlled Cuban cinema used the same tactic after the revolution of 1959.) In fact, during the abysmal years of the Russian Civil War (1918–20), nearly all Soviet films were *agitki* of some sort. Most of the great directors of the Soviet silent cinema were trained in that form, although, having very little technical equipment and no negative film stock, they were often required to make "films without celluloid."

Students at the VGIK were instructed to write, direct, and act out scenarios as if they were before cameras. Then—on paper—they assembled various "shots" into completed "films." The great teacher Lev Kuleshov obtained a print of Griffith's *Intolerance* and screened it for students in his "Kuleshov workshop" until they had memorized its shot structures and could rearrange its multilayered editing sequences on paper in hundreds of different combinations.

Kuleshov further experimented with editing by intercutting the same shot of a famous actor's expressionless face with several different shots of highly expressive content—a steaming bowl of soup, a dead woman in a coffin, and a little girl playing with a teddy bear. The invariable response of film school audiences when shown these sequences was that the actor's face assumed the emotion appropriate to the intercut object—hunger for the soup, sorrow for the dead woman, paternal affection for the little girl. Kuleshov reasoned from this phenomenon, known today as the "Kuleshov effect," that the shot in film always has two values: the one it carries in itself as a photographic image of reality and the one it acquires when placed into juxtaposition with another shot. He reasoned further that the second value is more important to cinematic signification than the first and that time and space in the cinema must therefore be subordinate to the process of editing, or "montage" (coined by the Soviets from the French verb *monter*, "to assemble"). Kuleshov ultimately conceived of montage as an expressive process whereby dissimilar images could be linked together to create nonliteral or symbolic meaning.

Although Kuleshov made several important films, including *Po zakonu* (*By the Law*, 1926), it was as a teacher and theorist that he most deeply influenced an entire generation of Soviet directors. Two of his most brilliant students were Sergey Eisenstein and Vsevolod Illarionovich Pudovkin.

Eisenstein was, with Griffith, one of the great pioneering geniuses of the modern cinema, and like his predecessor he produced a handful of enduring masterworks. Griffith, however, had elaborated the structure of narrative editing intuitively, whereas Eisenstein was an intellectual who formulated a modernist theory of editing based on the psychology of perception and Marxist dialectic. He was trained as a civil engineer, but in 1920 he joined the Moscow Proletkult Theatre, where he fell under the influence of the stage director Vsevolod Meyerhold and directed a number of plays in the revolutionary style of Futurism. In the winter of 1922–23 Eisenstein studied under Kuleshov and was inspired to write his first theoretical manifesto, "The Montage of Attractions," which advocated assaulting an audience with calculated emotional shocks for the purpose of agitation.

Eisenstein was invited to direct the Proletkult-sponsored film *Stachka* (*Strike*) in 1924, but, like Griffith, he knew little of the practical aspects of production. He therefore enlisted the aid of Eduard Tisse, a brilliant cinematographer at the state-owned Goskino studios, beginning a lifelong artistic collaboration. *Strike* is a semidocumentary representation of the brutal suppression of a strike by tsarist factory owners and police. In addition to being Eisenstein's first film, it was also the first revolutionary mass-film of the new Soviet state. Conceived as an extended montage of shock stimuli, the film concludes with the now famous sequence in which the massacre of the strikers and their families is intercut with shots of cattle being slaughtered in an abattoir.

Strike was an immediate success, and Eisenstein was next commissioned to direct a film celebrating the 20th anniversary of the failed 1905 Revolution against tsarism. Originally intended to provide a panorama of the entire event, the project eventually came to focus on a single representative episode—the mutiny of the battleship Potemkin and the massacre of the citizens of the port of Odessa by tsarist troops. *Bronenosets Potemkin* (*Battleship Potemkin*, 1925) emerged as one of the most important and influential films ever made, especially in Eisenstein's use of montage.

Although agitational to the core, *Battleship Potemkin* is a work of extraordinary pictorial beauty and great elegance of form. It is symmetrically broken into five movements or acts, according to the structure of Greek tragedy. In the first of these, "Men and Maggots," the flagrant mistreatment of the sailors at the hands of their officers is demonstrated, while the second, "Drama on the Quarterdeck," presents the actual mutiny and the ship's arrival in Odessa. "Appeal from the Dead" establishes the solidarity of the citizens of Odessa with the mutineers, but it is the fourth sequence, "The Odessa Steps," which depicts the massacre of the citizens, that thrust Eisenstein and his film into the historical eminence that both occupy today. Its power is such that the film's conclusion, "Meeting the Squadron," in which the Battleship Potemkin in a show of brotherhood is allowed to pass through the squadron unharmed, is anticlimactic.

Unquestionably the most famous sequence of its kind in film history, "The Odessa Steps" incarnates the theory of dialectical montage that Eisenstein later expounded in

Scene from "The Odessa Steps" sequence in the film *Battleship Potemkin* (1925), directed by Sergey Eisenstein.

his collected writings, *The Film Sense* (1942) and *Film Form* (1949). Eisenstein believed that meaning in motion pictures is generated by the collision of opposing shots. Building on Kuleshov's ideas, Eisenstein reasoned that montage operates according to the Marxist view of history as a perpetual conflict in which a force (thesis) and a counterforce (antithesis) collide to produce a totally new and greater phenomenon (synthesis). He compared this dialectical process in film editing to "the series of explosions of an internal combustion engine, driving forward its automobile or tractor." The force of "The Odessa Steps" arises when the viewer's mind combines individual, independent shots and forms a new, distinct conceptual impression that far outweighs the shots' narrative significance. Through Eisenstein's accelerated manipulations of filmic time and space, the slaughter on the stone steps—where hundreds of citizens find themselves trapped between descending tsarist militia above and Cossacks below—acquires a powerful symbolic meaning. With the addition of a stirring revolutionary score by the German Marxist composer Edmund Meisel, the agitational appeal of *Battleship Potemkin* became nearly irresistible, and, when exported in early 1926, it made Eisenstein world-famous.

Eisenstein's next project, *Oktyabr* (*October*, 1928), was commissioned by the Central Committee to commemorate the 10th anniversary of the Bolshevik Revolution. Accordingly, vast resources, including the Soviet army and navy, were placed at the director's disposal. Eisenstein based the shooting script on voluminous documentary material from the era and on John Reed's book *Ten Days That Shook the World*. When the film was completed in November 1927, it was just under four hours long. While Eisenstein was making *October*, however,

Joseph Stalin had taken control of the Politburo from Leon Trotsky, and the director was forced to cut the print by one-third to eliminate references to the exiled Trotsky.

Eisenstein had consciously used *October* as a laboratory for experimenting with "intellectual" or "ideological" montage, an abstract type of editing in which the relationships established between shots are conceptual rather than visual or emotional. When the film was finally released, however, Stalinist critics attacked this alleged "formalist excess" (aestheticism or elitism). The same charge was leveled even more bitterly against Eisenstein's next film, *Staroe i novoe* (*Old and New*, 1929), which Stalinist bureaucrats completely disavowed. Stalin hated Eisenstein because he was an intellectual and a Jew, but the director's international stature was such that he could not be publicly purged. Instead, Stalin used the Soviet state-subsidy apparatus to foil Eisenstein's projects and attack his principles at every turn, a situation that resulted in the director's failure to complete another film until *Alexander Nevsky* was commissioned in 1938.

Eisenstein's nearest rival in the Soviet silent cinema was his fellow student Vsevolod Illarionovich Pudovkin. Like Eisenstein, Pudovkin developed a new theory of montage, but one based on cognitive linkage rather than dialectical collision. He maintained that "the film is not shot, but built, built up from the separate strips of celluloid that are its raw material." Pudovkin, like Griffith, most often used montage for narrative rather than symbolic purpose. His films are more personal than Eisenstein's; the epic drama that is the focus of Eisenstein's films exists in Pudovkin's films merely to provide a backdrop for the interplay of human emotions.

Pudovkin's major work is *Mat* (*Mother*, 1926), a tale of strikebreaking and terrorism in which a woman loses first her husband and then her son to the opposing sides of the 1905 Revolution. The film was internationally acclaimed for the innovative intensity of its montage, as well as for its emotion and lyricism. Pudovkin's later films include *Konets Sankt-Peterburga* (*The End of St. Petersburg*, 1927), which, like Eisenstein's *October*, was commissioned to celebrate the 10th anniversary of the Bolshevik Revolution, and *Potomok Chingis-Khana* (*The Heir to Genghis Khan*, or *Storm over Asia*, 1928), which is set in Central Asia during the Russian Civil War. Both mingle human drama with the epic and the symbolic as they tell a story of a politically naive person who is galvanized into action by tsarist tyranny. Although Pudovkin was never persecuted as severely by the Stalinists as Eisenstein, he too was publicly charged with formalism for his experimental sound film *Prostoi sluchai* (*A Simple Case*, 1932), which he was forced to release without its sound track. Pudovkin made several more sound films but remains best known for his silent work.

Two other seminal figures of the Soviet silent era were Aleksandr Dovzhenko and Dziga Vertov (original name Denis Kaufman). Dovzhenko, the son of Ukrainian peasants, had been a political cartoonist and painter before becoming a director at the state-controlled Odessa studios in 1926. After several minor works, he made *Zvenigora* (1928), a collection of boldly stylized tales about a hunt for an ancient Scythian treasure set during four different stages of Ukrainian history; *Arsenal* (1929), an epic film poem about the effects of revolution and civil war upon the Ukraine; and *Zemlya* (*Earth*, 1930), which is considered to be his masterpiece. *Earth* tells the story of the conflict between a family of wealthy landowning peasants (*kulaks*) and the young peasants of a collective farm in a small Ukrainian village, but the film is less a narrative than a lyric hymn to the cyclic recurrence of birth, life, love, and death in nature and in humankind. Although the film is acclaimed today, when it was released, Stalinist critics denounced it as counterrevolutionary. Soon after, Dovzhenko entered a period of political eclipse, during which, however, he continued to make films.

Dziga Vertov (a pseudonym meaning "spinning top") was an artist of quite different talents. He began his career as an *agitki* photographer and newsreel editor and is now acknowledged as the father of cinema verité (a self-consciously realistic documentary movement of the 1960s and '70s) for his development and practice of the theory of the *kino-glaz* ("cinema-eye"). Vertov articulated this doctrine in the early 1920s in a number of radical manifestos in which he denounced conventional narrative cinema as impotent and demanded that it be replaced with a cinema of actuality based on the "organization of camera-recorded documentary material." Between 1922 and 1925, he put his idea into practice in a series of 23 carefully crafted newsreel-documentaries entitled *Kino-pravda* ("film truth") and *Goskinokalender*. Vertov's most famous film is *Chelovek's kinoapparatom* (*Man with a Movie Camera*, 1929), a feature-length portrait of Moscow from dawn to dusk. The film plays upon the "city symphony" genre inaugurated by Walter Ruttmann's *Berlin, the Symphony of a Great City* (1927), but Vertov repeatedly draws attention to the filmmaking process to create an autocritique of cinema itself.

Unlike most of his contemporaries, Vertov welcomed the coming of sound, envisioning it as a "radio-ear" to accompany the "cinema-eye." His first sound film, *Entuziazm—simfoniya Donbassa* (*Symphony of the Donbas*, 1931), was an extraordinary contribution to the new medium, as was *Tri pesni o Lenine* (*Three Songs*

About Lenin, 1934), yet Vertov could not escape the charge of formalist error any more than his peers. Although he did make the feature film *Kolybelnaya* (*Lullaby*) in 1937, for the most part the Stalinist establishment reduced him to the status of a newsreel photographer after 1934.

Many other Soviet filmmakers played important roles in the great decade of experiment that followed the Revolution, among them Grigory Kozintsev and Leonid Trauberg, Boris Barnet, Yakov Protazanov, Olga Preobrazhenskaya, Abram Room, and the documentarian Esther Shub. The period came to an abrupt end in 1929, when Stalin removed the state film trust (then called Sovkino) from the jurisdiction of the Commissariat of Education and placed it under the direct authority of the Supreme Council of the National Economy. Reorganized as Soyuzkino, the trust was turned over to the reactionary bureaucrat Boris Shumyatsky, a proponent of the narrowly ideological doctrine known as Socialist Realism. This policy, which came to dominate the Soviet arts, dictated that individual creativity be subordinated to the political aims of the party and the state. In practice, it militated against the symbolic, the experimental, and the avant-garde in favour of a literal-minded "people's art" that glorified representative Soviet heroes and idealized Soviet experience. The restraints imposed made it impossible for the great filmmakers of the postrevolutionary era to produce creative or innovative work, and the Soviet cinema went into decline.

POST-WORLD WAR I AMERICAN CINEMA

During the 1920s in the United States, motion-picture production, distribution, and exhibition became a major national industry and movies perhaps the major national obsession. The salaries of stars reached monumental proportions; filmmaking practices and narrative formulas were standardized to accommodate mass production; and Wall Street began to invest heavily in every branch of the business. The growing industry was organized according to the studio system that, in many respects, the producer Thomas Harper Ince had developed between 1914 and 1918 at Inceville, his studio in the Santa Ynez Canyon near Hollywood. Ince functioned as the central authority over multiple production units, each headed by a director who was required to shoot an assigned film according to a detailed continuity script. Every project was carefully budgeted and tightly scheduled, and Ince himself supervised the final cut. This central producer system was the prototype for the studio system of the 1920s, and, with some modification, it prevailed as the dominant mode of Hollywood production for the next 40 years.

Virtually all the major film genres evolved and were codified during the 1920s, but none was more characteristic of the period than the slapstick comedy. This form was originated by Mack Sennett, who, at his Keystone Studios, produced countless one- and two-reel shorts and features (*Tillie's Punctured Romance*, 1914; *The Surf Girl*, 1916; *Teddy at the Throttle*, 1917) whose narrative logic was subordinated to fantastic, purely visual humour. An anarchic mixture of circus, vaudeville, burlesque, pantomime, and the chase, Sennett's Keystone comedies created a world of inspired madness and mayhem, and they employed the talents of such future stars as Charlie Chaplin, Harry Langdon, Roscoe ("Fatty") Arbuckle, Mabel Normand, and Harold Lloyd. Chaplin, for example, who had developed the persona of the "Little Tramp" at Keystone, went on to direct and star in a series of shorts produced by Essanay in 1915 (*The Tramp*, *A Night in the Show*) and Mutual between 1916 and 1917 (*The Vagabond*, *One A.M.*, *The Rink*, *Easy Street*). In 1917 he was offered an eight-film contract with First National that enabled him to establish his own studio. He directed his first feature there, the semiautobiographical *The Kid* (1921), but most of his First National films were two-reelers. In 1919 Chaplin, D.W. Griffith, Mary Pickford, and Douglas Fairbanks, the four most popular and powerful film artists of the time, jointly formed the United Artists Corporation in order to produce and distribute—and thereby retain artistic and

Charlie Chaplin (*left*) and Harry Myers (*centre*) in *City Lights* (1931), directed by Chaplin.

financial control over—their own films. Chaplin directed three silent features for United Artists: *A Woman of Paris* (1923), his great comic epic *The Gold Rush* (1925), and *The Circus* (1928), which was released after the introduction of sound into motion pictures. He later made several sound films, but the two most successful—his first two, *City Lights* (1931) and *Modern Times* (1936)—were essentially silent films with musical scores.

Buster Keaton possessed a kind of comic talent very different from Chaplin's, but both men were wonderfully subtle actors with a keen sense of the tragic often contained within the comic, and both were major directors of their period. Keaton, like Chaplin, was born into a theatrical family and began performing in vaudeville skits at a young age. Intrigued by the new film medium, he left the stage and worked for two years as a supporting comedian for Arbuckle's production company. In 1919 Keaton formed his own production company, where over the next four years he made 20 shorts (including *One Week*, 1920; *The Boat*, 1921; *Cops*, 1922; and *The Balloonatic*, 1923) that represent, with Chaplin's Mutual films, the acme of American slapstick comedy. A Keaton trademark was the "trajectory gag," in which perfect timing of acting, directing, and editing propels his film character through a geometric progression of complicated sight gags that seem impossibly dangerous but are still dramatically logical. Such routines inform all of Keaton's major features—*Our Hospitality* (1923), *Sherlock, Jr.* (1924), *The Navigator* (1924), *Seven Chances* (1925), and his masterpieces *The General* (1927) and *Steamboat Bill, Jr.* (1928).

Important but lesser silent comics were Lloyd, the team of Stan Laurel and Oliver Hardy, Langdon, and Arbuckle. Working at the Hal Roach Studios, Lloyd cultivated the persona of an earnest, sweet-tempered boy-next-door. He specialized in a variant of Keystone mayhem known as the "comedy of thrills," in which—as in Lloyd's most famous features, *Safety Last!* (1923) and *The Freshman* (1925)—an innocent protagonist finds himself placed in physical danger. Laurel and Hardy also worked for Roach. They made 27 silent two-reelers, including *Putting Pants on Philip* (1927) and *Liberty* (1929), and became even more popular in the 1930s in such sound films as

ROSCOE ("FATTY") ARBUCKLE

Roscoe ("Fatty") Arbuckle was at the centre of the most damaging scandal to affect American motion pictures during the silent era. In September 1921 the comedian and several friends hosted a weekend party in a San Francisco hotel. During the party a woman became ill, and she later died in a hospital of peritonitis. Amid the volatile social transformations of the post-World War I era, with issues such as immigration restriction and the national prohibition of alcoholic beverages deeply dividing the country, many had come to regard motion pictures as a disturbing instigator of social change and its high-living stars as threats to moral order and values. The Arbuckle scandal seemed to encapsulate these fears, and prosecutors responded by accusing the actor of rape and murder. Eventually indicted for manslaughter, he was tried three times; the first two trials ended in hung juries, and in the third the jury deliberated for six minutes and voted for acquittal. But Arbuckle's career as an actor was in ruins, and he was banned from the screen for more than a decade. Other sensational deaths involving Hollywood personalities, through murder or suicide or drug overdose, fueled the public furor.

Another Fine Mess (1930) and *Sons of the Desert* (1933). Their comic characters were basically grown-up children whose relationship was sometimes disturbingly sadomasochistic. Langdon also traded on a childlike, even babylike, image in such popular features as *The Strong Man* (1926) and *Long Pants* (1927), both directed by Frank Capra. Arbuckle, however, in his few years of stardom, created the character of a leering, sensual adult. Arbuckle's talent was limited, but his persona affected the course of American film history in a quite unexpected way.

To stave off increasing efforts by state and local governments to censor motion pictures, the Hollywood studios formed a new, stronger trade association, the Motion Picture Producers and Distributors of America (MPPDA; later renamed the Motion Picture Association of America). They also hired a conservative politician, U.S. Postmaster General Will H. Hays, as its head. The Hays Office, as the association became popularly known, advocated industry self-regulation as an alternative to governmental interference, and it succeeded in preventing the expansion of censorship efforts. Hays promulgated a series of documents that attempted to regulate various forms of criminal and immoral behaviour depicted in motion pictures. A principle such as "compensating values," for example, recognized that popular entertainment had always told stories of lawbreaking and social transgression, but it held that law and morality should always triumph in a film.

The leading practitioner of the compensating values formula was the flamboyant director Cecil B. DeMille. He first became famous after World War I for a series of sophisticated comedies of manners that were aimed at Hollywood's new middle-class audience (*Old Wives for New*, 1918; *Forbidden Fruit*, 1921). When the Hays Office was established, DeMille turned to the sex- and violence-drenched religious spectacles that made him an international figure, notably *The Ten Commandments* (1923; remade 1956). DeMille's chief rival in the production of stylish sex comedies was the German émigré Ernst Lubitsch. An early master of the UFA Kostümfilm, Lubitsch excelled at sexual innuendo and understatement in such urbane essays as *The Marriage Circle* (1924). Also popular during the 1920s were the swashbuckling exploits of Douglas Fairbanks, whose lavish adventure spectacles, including *Robin Hood* (1922) and *The Thief of Bagdad* (1924), thrilled a generation, and the narrative documentaries of Robert Flaherty, whose *Nanook of the North* (1922) and *Moana* (1926) were unexpectedly successful with the public and with critics.

The most enigmatic and unconventional figure working in Hollywood at the time, however, was without a doubt the Viennese émigré Erich von Stroheim. Stroheim, who also acted, learned directing as an assistant to Griffith on *Intolerance* and *Hearts of the World*. His first three films—*Blind Husbands* (1918), *The Devil's Passkey* (1919), and *Foolish Wives* (1922)—constitute an obsessive trilogy of adultery; each features a sexual triangle in which an American wife is seduced by a Prussian army officer. Even though all three films were enormously popular, the great sums Stroheim was spending on the extravagant production design and costuming of his next project brought him into conflict with his Universal producers, and he was replaced.

Stroheim then signed a contract with Goldwyn Pictures and began work on a long-cherished project—an adaptation of Frank Norris's grim naturalistic novel *McTeague*. Shot entirely on location in the streets and rooming houses of San Francisco, in Death Valley, and in the California hills, the film was conceived as a sentence-by-sentence translation of its source. Realizing that the film was too long to be exhibited (about 10 hours), Stroheim cut almost half the footage. The film was still deemed too long, so Stroheim, with the help of director Rex Ingram, edited it down into a four-hour version that could be shown in two parts. By that time, however, Goldwyn Pictures had merged with Metro Pictures and Louis B. Mayer Pictures to become MGM. MGM took the negative from Stroheim and cut another two hours, destroying

Pictured here are (*from left*) Zasu Pitts, Gibson Gowland, and Hughie Mack in the silent film *Greed* (1924), directed by Erich von Stroheim.

the excised footage in the process. Released as *Greed* (1924), the film had enormous gaps in continuity, but it was still recognized as a work of genius in its rich psychological characterization and in its creation of a naturalistic analogue for the novel.

Stroheim made one more film for MGM, a darkly satiric adaptation of the Franz Lehár operetta *The Merry Widow* (1925). He then went to Celebrity Pictures, where he directed

The Wedding March (1928), a two-part spectacle set in imperial Vienna, but his work was taken from him and recut into a single film when Celebrity was absorbed by Paramount. Stroheim's last directorial duties were on the botched *Queen Kelly* (1929) and *Walking down Broadway* (1932), although he was removed from both films for various reasons. He made his living thereafter by writing screenplays and acting.

Although many of Stroheim's troubles with Hollywood were personal, he was also a casualty of the American film industry's transformation during the 1920s from a speculative entrepreneurial enterprise into a vertically and horizontally integrated oligopoly that had no tolerance for creative difference. His situation was not unique; many singular artists, including Griffith, Sennett, Chaplin, and Keaton, found it difficult to survive as filmmakers under the rigidly standardized studio system that had been established by the end of the decade. The industry's conversion to sound at that time reinforced its big-business tendencies and further discouraged independent filmmakers. The studios, which had borrowed huge sums of money on the very brink of the Great Depression in order to finance the conversion, were determined to reduce production costs and increase efficiency. They therefore became less and less willing to tolerate artistic innovation or eccentricity.

CHAPTER THREE

THE PRE–WORLD WAR II SOUND ERA

The wholesale conversion to sound of all three sectors of the American film industry took place in less than 15 months between late 1927 and 1929, and the profits of the major companies increased during that period by as much as 600 percent. Although the transition was fast, orderly, and profitable, it was also enormously expensive. The industrial system as it had evolved for the previous three decades needed to be completely overhauled; studios and theatres had to be totally reequipped and creative personnel retrained or fired. In order to fund the conversion, the film companies were forced to borrow in excess of $350 million, which placed them under the indirect control of the two major New York-based financial groups, the Morgan group and the Rockefeller group.

Furthermore, although cooperation between the film companies through such agencies as the MPPDA, the Academy of Motion Picture Arts and Sciences, and the

Society of Motion Picture Engineers ensured a smooth transition in corporate terms, inside the newly wired theatres and studio soundstages there was confusion and disruption. The three competing systems—Vitaphone, Movietone, and Photophone—were all initially incompatible, and their technologies were under such constant modification that equipment was sometimes obsolete before it was uncrated. Whatever system producers chose, exhibitors during the early transitional period were forced to maintain both sound-on-disc and sound-on-film reproduction equipment. Even as late as 1931, studios were still releasing films in both formats to accommodate theatres owned by sound-on-disc interests.

It was in the area of production, however, that the greatest problems arose. The statement that "the movies ceased to move when they began to talk" accurately described the films made during the earliest years of the transition, largely because of technical limitations. Early microphones, for example, had a very limited range. In addition, they were large, clumsy, and difficult to move, so they were usually concealed in a single, stationary location on the set. The actors, who had to speak directly into the microphones to register on the sound track, were therefore forced to remain practically motionless while delivering dialogue. The microphones caused further problems because they were omnidirectional within their range and picked up every sound made near them on the set, especially the noisy whir of running cameras (which were motorized in 1929 to run at an even speed of 24 frames per second to ensure undistorted sound synchronization; silent cameras had been mainly hand-cranked at rates averaging 16 to 18 frames per second). To prevent the recording of camera noise, cameras and their operators were initially enclosed in soundproof glass-paneled booths that were only 6 feet (2 metres) long per side. The booths, which were facetiously called "iceboxes" because they were uncomfortably hot and stuffy, literally imprisoned the camera. The filmmakers' inability to tilt or dolly the camera (although they could pan it by as much as 30 degrees on its tripod), combined with the actors' immobility, helps to account for the static nature of so many early sound films.

The impact of sound recording on editing was even more regressive, because sound and image had to be recorded simultaneously to be synchronous. In sound-on-disc films, scenes were initially made to play for 10 minutes at a time in order to record dialogue continuously on 16-inch (41-cm) discs; such scenes were impossible to edit until the technology of rerecording was perfected in the early 1930s. Sound-on-film systems also militated against editing at first; optical sound tracks run approximately 20 frames in advance of their corresponding image tracks, making it extremely difficult to cut a composite print without eliminating portions of the relevant sound. As a result, no matter which system of sound recording was used, most of the editing in early sound films was purely functional. In general, cuts could be made—and the camera moved—only when no sound was being recorded on the set.

Most of these technical problems were resolved by 1933, although equilibrium was not fully restored to the production process until after the mid-1930s. Sound-on-disc filming, for example, was abandoned in 1930, and by 1931 all the studios had removed their cameras from the iceboxes and converted to the use of lightweight soundproof camera housings known as "blimps." Within several years, smaller, quieter, self-insulating cameras were produced, eliminating the need for external soundproofing altogether. It even became possible again to move the camera by using a wide range of boom cranes, camera supports, and steerable dollies. Microphones too became increasingly mobile as a variety of booms were developed for them from 1930 onward. These long radial arms suspended the microphone above the set, allowing it to follow the movements of actors and rendering the stationary microphones of the early years obsolete.

Microphones also became more directional throughout the decade, and track noise-suppression techniques came into use as early as 1931.

POSTSYNCHRONIZATION

The technological development that most liberated the sound film, however, was the practice known variously as postsynchronization, rerecording, or dubbing, in which image and sound are printed on separate pieces of film so that they can be manipulated independently. Postsynchronization enabled filmmakers to edit images freely again. Because the overwhelming emphasis of the period from 1928 to 1931 had been on obtaining high-quality sound in production, however, the idea that the sound track could be modified after it was recorded took a while to catch on. Many motion-picture artists and technicians felt that sound should be reproduced in films exactly as it had originally been produced on the set; they believed that anything less than an absolute pairing of sound and image would confuse audiences.

For several years, both practice and ideology dictated that sound and image be recorded simultaneously, so that everything heard on the sound track would be seen on the screen and vice versa. A vocal minority of film artists nevertheless viewed this practice of synchronous, "naturalistic" sound recording as a threat to the cinema. In their 1928 manifesto "Sound and Image," the Soviet directors Sergey Eisenstein, Vsevolod Pudovkin, and Grigory Aleksandrov denounced synchronous sound in favour of asynchronous, contrapuntal sound—sound that would counterpoint the images it accompanied to become another dynamic element in the montage process. Like the practical editing problem, the theoretical debate over the appropriate use of sound was eventually resolved by the practice of postsynchronization.

Postsynchronization seems to have first been used by the American director King Vidor for a sequence in which the hero is chased through Arkansas swamplands in the all-black musical *Hallelujah* (1929). Vidor shot the action on location without sound, using a freely moving camera. Later, in the studio, he added to the film a separately recorded sound track containing both naturalistic and impressionistic effects. In the following year Lewis Milestone's *All Quiet on the Western Front* and G.W. Pabst's *Westfront 1918* both used postsynchronization for their battle scenes. Ernst Lubitsch used dubbing in his first American sound films, the dynamic musicals *The Love Parade* (1929) and *Monte Carlo* (1930), as did the French director René Clair in *Sous les toits de Paris* (*Under the*

Roofs of Paris, 1930). In all these early instances, sound was recorded and rerecorded on a single track, although some American directors, including Milestone and the Russian-born Armenian Rouben Mamoulian (*Applause*, 1929; *City Streets*, 1931), had experimented with multiple microphone setups and overlapping dialogue as early as 1929. Generally, through 1932, either dialogue or music dominated the sound track unless they had been simultaneously recorded on the set. In 1933, however, technology was introduced that allowed filmmakers to mix separately recorded tracks for background music, sound effects, and synchronized dialogue at the dubbing stage. By the late 1930s, postsynchronization and multiple-channel mixing had become standard industry procedure.

NONTECHNICAL EFFECTS OF SOUND

Other changes wrought by sound were more purely human. Directors, for example, could no longer literally direct their performers while the cameras were rolling and sound was being recorded. Actors and actresses were suddenly required to have pleasant voices and to act without the assistance of mood music or the director's shouted instructions through long dialogue takes. Many found that they could not learn lines; others tried and were defeated by heavy foreign accents (e.g., Emil Jannings, Pola Negri, Vilma Banky, and Lya de Putti) or voices that did not match their screen image (e.g., Colleen Moore, Corinne Griffith, Norma Talmadge, and John Gilbert). Numerous silent stars were supplanted during the transitional period by stage actors or film actors with stage experience. "Canned theatre," or literal transcriptions of stage hits, became a dominant Hollywood form between 1929 and 1931, which brought many Broadway players and directors into the film industry on a more or less permanent basis. In addition, to fulfill the unprecedented need for dialogue scripts, the studios imported hundreds of editors, critics, playwrights, and novelists, many of whom would make lasting contributions to the verbal sophistication of the American sound film.

As sound demanded new filmmaking techniques and talents, it also created new genres and renovated old ones. The realism it permitted inspired the emergence of tough, socially pertinent films with urban settings. Crime epics, or gangster films, such

Actor Edward G. Robinson in a promotional portrait for *Little Caesar*, directed by Mervyn LeRoy, 1931.

as Mervyn LeRoy's *Little Caesar* (1931), William Wellman's *Public Enemy* (1931), and Howard Hawks's *Scarface* (1932), used sound to exploit urban slang and the audible pyrotechnics of the recently invented Thompson submachine gun. Subgenres of the gangster film were the prison film (e.g., *The Big House*, 1930; Hawks's *The Criminal Code*, 1931; LeRoy's *I Am a Fugitive from a Chain Gang*, 1932) and the newspaper picture (e.g., Milestone's *The Front Page*, 1931; LeRoy's *Five Star Final*, 1931; John Cromwell's *Scandal Sheet*, 1931; Frank Capra's *Platinum Blonde*, 1931), both of which relied on authentic-sounding vernacular speech.

The public's fascination with speech also accounted for the new popularity of historical biographies, or "biopics." These films were modeled on the Universersum Film AG's (UFA's) silent *Kostümfilm*, but dialogue enhanced their verisimilitude. Several actors with impressive speaking voices were often associated with the genre, notably George Arliss (*Disraeli*, 1929; *The House of Rothschild*, 1934) and Paul Muni (*The Life of Emile Zola*, 1937; *Juarez*, 1939) in the United States and Charles Laughton (Alexander Korda's *The Private Life of Henry VIII*, 1933; *Rembrandt*, 1936) in England.

In the realm of comedy, pure slapstick could not and did not survive, predicated as it was on purely visual humour. It was replaced by equally vital—but ultimately less surreal and abstract—sound comedies: the anarchic dialogue comedies of the Marx Brothers (*The Cocoanuts*, 1929; *Animal Crackers*, 1930; *Monkey Business*, 1931; *Horse Feathers*, 1932; *Duck Soup*, 1933) and W.C. Fields (*The Golf Specialist*, 1930; *The Dentist*, 1932; *Million Dollar Legs*, 1932) and the fast-paced wisecracking "screwball" comedies of directors such as Capra (*Lady for a Day*, 1933; *It Happened One Night*, 1934; *Mr. Deeds Goes to Town*, 1936), Hawks (*Twentieth Century*, 1934; *Bringing Up Baby*, 1938), Gregory La Cava (*My Man Godfrey*, 1936), Mitchell Leisen (*Easy Living*, 1937), and Leo McCarey (*The Awful Truth*, 1937).

The horror-fantasy genre, traditionally rooted in German Expressionism, was greatly enhanced by sound, which not only permitted the addition of eerie sound effects but also restored the dimension of literary dialogue present in so many of the original sources. Appropriately, Universal Pictures' three great horror classics—Tod Browning's *Dracula* (1931), James Whale's *Frankenstein* (1931), and Karl Freund's *The Mummy* (1932)—were all early sound films.

One significant genre whose emergence was obviously contingent upon sound was the musical. Versions of Broadway musicals were among the first sound films made (including, of course, the catalyst for the conversion, Warner Brothers' *The Jazz Singer*), and by the early 1930s the movie musical had developed in formal sophistication to become perhaps the major American genre of the decade. Among the formidable artists who helped to achieve this sophistication were director Ernst Lubitsch at Paramount (*The Love Parade*, 1929; *Monte Carlo*, 1930; *The Smiling Lieutenant*, 1931), dance director Busby Berkeley at Warner Brothers (*42nd Street*, 1933; *Gold Diggers of 1933*, 1933; *Footlight Parade*, 1933; *Dames*, 1934), and dancer-star Fred Astaire, who choreographed and directed his own integrated dance sequences at RKO (*The Gay Divorcee*, 1934; *Roberta*, 1935; *Top Hat*, 1935; *Swing Time*, 1936). Ginger Rogers was Astaire's dancing partner in these and six other films during the 1930s.

Walt Disney pioneered a genre that might be called the animated musical with *The Skeleton Dance* (1929), the first entry in his "Silly Symphony" series. Unburdened by the awkward logistics of live-action shooting, Disney was free to combine sound and image asynchronously or with perfect frame-by-frame synchronization in such classic cartoons as *Steamboat Willie* (1928—Mickey Mouse's debut) and *The Three Little Pigs* (1933). To enhance their fantasy-like appeal, both the musical and the animated film made early use of the two-colour imbibition process introduced by the Technicolor Corporation in 1928, during the conversion to sound. Animated films also pioneered the use of Technicolor's three-colour, three-strip imbibition process, introduced in 1932.

INTRODUCTION OF COLOUR

Photographic colour entered the cinema at approximately the same time as sound, although, as with sound, various colour effects had been used in films since the invention of the medium. Georges Méliès, for example, employed 21 women at his Montreuil studio to hand-colour his films frame by frame, but hand-colouring was not cost-effective unless films were very short. In the mid-1900s, as films began to approach one reel in length and more prints of each film were sold, mechanized stenciling processes were introduced. In Pathé's Pathécolor system, for example, a stencil was cut for each colour desired (up to six) and aligned with the print; colour was then applied through the stencil frame by frame at high speeds. With the advent of the feature and the conversion of the industry to mass production during the 1910s, frame-by-frame stenciling was replaced by mechanized tinting and toning. Tinting coloured all the light areas of a picture and was achieved by immersing a black-and-white print in dye or by using coloured film base for printing. The toning process involved chemically treating film emulsion to colour the dark areas of the print. Each

(continued on the next page)

(*continued from the previous page*)

process produced monochrome images, the colour of which was usually chosen to correspond to the mood or setting of the scene. Occasionally, the two processes were combined to produce elaborate two-colour effects. By the early 1920s, nearly all American features included at least one coloured sequence; but after 1927, when it was discovered that tinting or toning film stock interfered with the transmission of optical sound, both practices were temporarily abandoned, leaving the market open to new systems of colour photography.

Photographic colour can be produced in motion pictures by using either an additive process or a subtractive one. The first systems to be developed and used were all additive ones, such as Charles Urban's Kinemacolor (c. 1906) and Gaumont's Chronochrome (c. 1912). They achieved varying degrees of popularity, but none was entirely successful, largely because all additive systems involve the use of both special cameras and projectors, which ultimately makes them too complicated and costly for widespread industrial use.

One of the first successful subtractive processes was a two-colour one introduced by Herbert Kalmus's Technicolor Corporation in 1922. It used a special camera and a complex procedure to produce two separate positive prints that were then cemented together into a single print. The final print needed careful handling but could be projected by means of ordinary equipment. This "cemented positive" process was used successfully in such features as *Toll of the Sea* (1922) and Fairbanks's *The Black Pirate* (1926). In 1928 Technicolor introduced an improved process in which two gelatin positives were used as relief matrices to "print" colour onto a single strip of film. This printing process, known as imbibition, or dye-transfer, made it possible to mass-produce sturdy, high-quality prints. Its introduction resulted in a significant rise in Technicolor production between 1929 and 1932. Colour reproduction in the two-colour Technicolor process was good, but, because only two of the three primary colours were used, it was still not completely lifelike. Its popularity began to decline sharply in 1932, and Technicolor replaced it with a three-colour system that employed the same basic principles but included all three primary colours.

For the next 25 years almost every colour film made was produced by using Technicolor's three-colour system. Although the quality of the system was excellent,

(continued on the next page)

(*continued from the previous page*)

there were drawbacks. The bulk of the camera made location shooting difficult. Furthermore, Technicolor's virtual monopoly gave it indirect control of the production companies, which were required to rent—at high rates—equipment, crew, consultants, and laboratory services from Technicolor every time they used the system. In the midst of the Depression, therefore, conversion to colour was slow and never really complete. After three-colour Technicolor was used successfully in Disney's cartoon short *The Three Little Pigs* (1933), the live-action short *La Cucaracha* (1934), and Rouben Mamoulian's live-action feature *Becky Sharp* (1935), it gradually worked its way into mainstream feature production (*The Garden of Allah*, 1936; *Snow White and the Seven Dwarfs*, 1937; *The Adventures of Robin Hood*, 1938; *The Wizard of Oz*, 1939; *Gone with the Wind*, 1939), although it remained strongly associated with fantasy and spectacle.

A scene from *The Wizard of Oz* (1939), directed by Victor Fleming.

THE HOLLYWOOD STUDIO SYSTEM

If the coming of sound changed the aesthetic dynamics of the filmmaking process, it altered the economic structure of the industry even more, precipitating some of the largest mergers in motion-picture history. Throughout the 1920s, Paramount, MGM, First National, and other studios had conducted ambitious campaigns of vertical integration by ruthlessly acquiring first-run theatre chains. It was primarily in response to those aggressive maneuvers that Warner Brothers and Fox sought to dominate smaller exhibitors by providing prerecorded musical accompaniment to their films. The unexpected success of their strategy forced the industrywide conversion to sound and transformed Warner Brothers and Fox into major corporations. By 1929, Warner Brothers had acquired the Stanley theatre circuit, which controlled nearly all the first-run houses in the mid-Atlantic states, and the production and distribution facilities of its former rival First National to become one of the largest studios in Hollywood. Fox went even farther, building the multimillion-dollar Movietone City in Westwood, Calif., in 1928 and acquiring controlling shares of both Loew's, Inc., the parent corporation of MGM, and Gaumont British, England's largest producer-distributor-exhibitor. Its holdings were surpassed only by those of Paramount, which controlled an international distribution network and the vast Publix theatre chain. In an effort to become even more powerful, Paramount in 1929 acquired one-half of the newly formed Columbia Broadcasting System and proposed a merger with Warner Brothers. It was then that the U.S. Department of Justice intervened, forbidding Paramount's merger with Warner Brothers and divorcing Fox from Loew's.

Without government interference, "Paramount-Vitaphone" and "Fox-Loew's" might have divided the entertainment industries of the entire English-speaking world between them. As it was, by 1930, 95 percent of all American production was concentrated in the hands of only eight studios—five vertically integrated major companies, which controlled production, distribution, and exhibition, and three horizontally integrated minor ones that controlled production and distribution. Distribution was conducted at both a national and an international level: since about 1925, foreign rentals had accounted for half of all American feature revenues, and they would continue to do so for the next two decades. Exhibition was controlled through the major studios' ownership of 2,600 first-run theatres, which represented 16 percent of the national total but generated three-fourths of the revenue. Film production throughout the 1930s and '40s consumed only 5 percent of total corporate assets, while distribution accounted for another 1 percent. The remaining 94 percent of the studios' investment went to the exhibition sector. In short, as film historian Douglas Gomery pointed out, the five major studios of the time can best be characterized as "diversified theater chains, producing features, shorts, cartoons, and newsreels to fill their houses."

Each studio produced a distinctive style of entertainment, depending on its corporate economy and the personnel it had under contract. MGM, the largest and most powerful of the major studios, was also the most "American" and was given to the celebration of middle-class values in a visual style characterized by bright, even, high-key lighting and opulent production design. Paramount, with its legions of UFA-trained directors, art directors, and cameramen, was thought to be the most "European" of the studios. It produced the most sophisticated and visually baroque films of the era. Conditioned by its recent experience as a struggling minor studio, Warner Brothers was the most cost-conscious of the major companies. Its directors worked on a quota system, and a flat, low-key lighting style was decreed by the studio to conceal the cheapness of its sets. Warner Brothers' films were often targeted for working-class audiences. Twentieth Century-Fox acquired a reputation for its tight budget and production control, but its films were noted for their glossy attractiveness and state-of-the-art special effects. RKO Radio was the smallest of the major companies and never achieved complete financial stability during the studio era; it became prominent, however, as the producer of *King Kong* (1933), the Astaire-Rogers dance cycle, and Orson Welles's *Citizen Kane* (1941) and also as the distributor of Disney's features.

The minor studios were Carl Laemmle's Universal Pictures, which became justly famous for its horror films; Harry Cohn's Columbia Pictures, whose main assets were director Frank Capra and screenwriter Robert Riskin; and United Artists, which functioned as a distributor for independent American features and for Alexander Korda's London Film Productions. At the very bottom of the film industry hierarchy were a score of poorly capitalized studios, such as Republic, Monogram, and Grand National, that produced cheap formulaic hour-long "B movies" for the second half of double bills. The double feature, an attraction introduced in the early 1930s to counter the Depression-era box-office slump, was the standard form of exhibition for about 15 years. The larger studios were, for the most part, not interested in producing B movies for double bills, because, unlike the main feature, whose earnings were based on box-office receipts, the second feature rented at a flat rate, which meant that the profit it returned, though guaranteed, was fixed at a small amount. At their peak, the B-film studios produced 40–50 movies per year and provided a training ground for such stars as John Wayne. The films were made as quickly as possible, and directors functioned as their own producers, with complete authority over their projects' minuscule budgets.

An important aspect of the studio system was the Production Code, which was implemented in 1934 in response to pressure from the Legion of Decency and public protest against the graphic violence and sexual suggestiveness of some sound films (the urban gangster films, for example, and the films of Mae West). The Legion had been established in 1933 by the American bishops of the Roman Catholic church (armed with a mandate from the Vatican) to fight for better and more "moral" motion pictures. In April 1934, with the support of both Protestant and Jewish organizations, the Legion called for a nationwide boycott of movies it considered indecent. The studios, having lost millions of dollars in 1933 as the delayed effects of the Depression caught up with the box office, rushed to appease the protesters by authorizing the MPPDA to create the Production Code Administration. A prominent Catholic layman, Joseph I. Breen, was appointed to head the administration, and under Breen's auspices Father Daniel A. Lord, a Jesuit priest, and Martin Quigley, a Catholic publisher, coauthored

PRODUCTION CODE

In a swing away from the excesses of the "new morality" of the Jazz Age, the Production Code was monumentally repressive, forbidding the depiction on-screen of almost everything germane to the experience of normal human adults. It prohibited showing "scenes of passion," and adultery, illicit sex, seduction, and rape could not even be alluded to unless they were absolutely essential to the plot and severely punished by the film's end. The code demanded that the sanctity of marriage be upheld at all times, although sexual relations were not to be suggested between spouses. It forbade the use of profanity, vulgarity, and racial epithets; prostitution, miscegenation, sexual deviance, or drug addiction; nudity, sexually suggestive dancing or costumes, and "lustful kissing"; and excessive drinking, cruelty to animals or children, and the representation of surgical operations, especially childbirth, "in fact or silhouette." In the realm of violence, it was forbidden to display or to discuss contemporary weapons, to show the details of a crime, to show law-enforcement officers dying

(continued on the next page)

(continued from the previous page)

at the hands of criminals, to suggest excessive brutality or slaughter, or to use murder or suicide except when crucial to the plot. Finally, the code required that all criminal activity be shown to be punished; under no circumstances could any crime be represented as justified. Studios were required to submit their scripts to Breen's office for approval before beginning filming, and completed films had to be screened for the office, and altered if necessary, in order to receive a Production Code Seal, without which no film could be distributed in the United States. Noncompliance with the code's restrictions brought a fine of $25,000, but the studios were so eager to please that the fine was never levied in the 22-year lifetime of the code.

the code whose provisions would dictate the content of American motion pictures, without exception, for the next 20 years.

The studio heads were willing not merely to accept but also to institutionalize this system of de facto censorship and prior restraint because they believed it was necessary for the continued success of their business. The economic threat of a national boycott during the worst years of the Depression was real, and the film industry, which depends on pleasing a mass audience, could not afford to ignore public opinion. Producers found, moreover, that they could use the code to increase the efficiency of production. By rigidly prescribing and proscribing the kinds of behaviour that could be shown or described on the screen, the code could be used as a scriptwriter's blueprint. A love story, for example, could move in only one direction (toward marriage); adultery and crime could have only one conclusion (disease or horrible death); dialogue in all situations had well-defined parameters; and so forth. The code, in other words, provided a framework for the construction of screenplays and enabled studios to streamline what had always been (and still is) one of the most difficult and yet most essential tasks in the production process—the creation of filmable continuity scripts. Furthermore, the Depression was a time of open political anti-Semitism in the United States, and the men who controlled the American motion-picture industry were mainly Jewish; it was not a propitious moment for them to antagonize their predominantly non-Jewish audience.

Between 1930 and 1945, the studio system produced more than 7,500 features, every stage of which, from conception through exhibition, was carefully controlled. Among these assembly-line productions are some of the most important American films ever made, the work of gifted directors who managed to transcend the mechanistic nature of the system to produce work of unique personal vision. These directors include Josef von Sternberg, whose exotically stylized films starring Marlene Dietrich (*Shanghai Express*, 1932; *The Scarlet Empress*, 1934) constitute a kind of painting with light; John Ford, whose vision of history as moral truth produced such mythic works as *Stagecoach* (1939), *Young Mr. Lincoln* (1939), *The Grapes of Wrath* (1940), *My Darling Clementine* (1946), and *She Wore a Yellow Ribbon* (1949); Howard Hawks, a master of genres and the architect of a tough, functional "American" style of narrative exemplified in his films *Scarface* (1932), *Twentieth Century* (1934), *Only Angels Have Wings* (1939), and *The Big Sleep* (1946); British émigré Alfred Hitchcock, whose films appealed to the popular audience as suspense melodramas but were in fact abstract visual psychodramas of guilt and spiritual terror (*Rebecca*, 1940; *Suspicion*, 1941; *Shadow of a Doubt*, 1943; *Notorious*, 1946); and Frank Capra, whose cheerful screwball comedies (*It Happened One Night*, 1934) and populist fantasies of good will (*Mr. Smith Goes

to Washington, 1939) sometimes gave way to darker warnings against losing faith and integrity (*It's a Wonderful Life*, 1946). Other significant directors with less-consistent thematic or visual

Alfred Hitchcock (*centre*) and George Sanders (*right*) in *Rebecca* (1940).

styles were William Wyler (*Wuthering Heights*, 1939; *The Little Foxes*, 1941), George Cukor (*Camille*, 1936; *The Philadelphia Story*, 1940), Leo McCarey (*The Awful Truth*, 1937; *Going My Way*, 1944), Preston Sturges (*Sullivan's Travels*, 1941; *The Miracle of Morgan's Creek*, 1944), and George Stevens (*Gunga Din*, 1939; *Woman of the Year*, 1942).

The most extraordinary film to emerge from the studio system, however, was Orson Welles's *Citizen Kane* (1941), whose controversial theme and experimental technique combined to make it a classic. The first of six films Welles had contracted to produce for RKO with his Mercury Theater radio ensemble company, Citizen Kane made radically innovative use of sound and deep-focus photography as it examined the life of Charles Foster Kane, a character based on the press baron William Randolph Hearst. The film employs a complicated flashback structure in

Orson Welles as Charles Foster Kane in *Citizen Kane* (1941), which Welles also directed.

which Kane's friends and associates give their accounts of the man after his death, paradoxically revealing not greatness or might but pathetic insecurity and emptiness. In creating this portrait of a powerful American who could bend international politics to his will but never fathom human love, Welles stretched the technology of image and sound recording beyond its contemporary limits. Using a newly available Eastman film stock with increased sensitivity to light, plastic-coated wide-angle lenses opened to smaller-than-normal apertures, and high-intensity arc lamps, cinematographer Gregg Toland achieved a photographic depth of field that approximated the perceptual range of the human eye and enabled Welles to place the film's characters in several different planes of depth within a single scene. These deep-focus sequence shots are complemented throughout the film by the techniques of ambient and directional sound that Welles had learned from radio. Most important of all, the resonance of the film's narrative matches the technical brilliance of its presentation, functioning on several levels at once: the historical, the psychological, and the mythic. Although recognized by many critics as a work of genius, *Citizen Kane* was a financial failure on its release, and Welles directed only three other films under his RKO contract. *Citizen Kane* remains, nevertheless, one of the most influential films ever made and is widely considered to be one of the greatest.

INTERNATIONAL CINEMA

Having created large new markets for their sound-recording technologies in the United States, Western Electric and RCA were eager to do the same abroad. Their objective coincided with the desire of the major American film studios to extend their control of the international motion-picture industry. Accordingly, the studios began to export sound films in late 1928, and ERPI and RCA began installing their equipment in European theatres at the same time. Exhibitors in the United Kingdom converted the most rapidly, with 22 percent wired for sound in 1929 and 63 percent by the end of 1932. Continental exhibitors converted more slowly, largely because of a bitter patents war between the German cartel Tobis-Klangfilm, which controlled the European rights to sound-on-film technology, and Western Electric. The dispute was finally resolved at the 1930 German-American Film Conference in Paris, where Tobis, ERPI, and RCA agreed to pool their patents and divide the world market among themselves. The language problem also delayed the conversion to sound on the Continent. Because dubbing was all but impossible in the earliest years of the transition, films had to be shot in several different languages (sometimes featuring a different cast for each version) at the time of production in order to receive wide international distribution. Paramount therefore built a huge studio in the Paris suburb of Joinville in 1930 to mass-produce multilingual films. The other major American studios quickly followed suit, making the region a factory for the round-the-clock production of movies in as many as 15 separate languages. By the end of 1931, however, the technique of dubbing had been sufficiently perfected to replace multilingual production, and Joinville was converted into a dubbing centre for all of Europe.

CHAPTER FOUR

DECLINE OF THE HOLLYWOOD STUDIOS: THE WAR YEARS AND POST-WORLD WAR II TRENDS

During the U.S. involvement in World War II, the Hollywood film industry cooperated closely with the government to support its war-aims information campaign. Following the declaration of war on Japan, the government created a Bureau of Motion Picture Affairs to coordinate the production of entertainment features with patriotic, morale-boosting themes and messages about the "American way of life," the nature of the enemy and the allies, civilian responsibility on the home front, and the fighting forces themselves. Initially unsophisticated vehicles for xenophobia and jingoism with titles such as *The Devil with Hitler* and *Blondie for Victory* (both 1942), Hollywood's wartime films became increasingly serious as the war dragged on (Fritz Lang's *Hangmen Also Die*, Jean Renoir's *This Land Is Mine*,

Tay Garnett's *Bataan*, all 1943; Delmer Daves's *Destination Tokyo*, Alfred Hitchcock's *Lifeboat*, Lewis Milestone's *The Purple Heart*, all 1944; Milestone's *A Walk in the Sun*, 1946). In addition to commercial features, several Hollywood directors produced documentaries for government and military agencies. Among the best-known of these films, which were designed to explain the war to both servicemen and civilians, are Frank Capra's seven-part series *Why We Fight* (1942–44), John Ford's *The Battle of Midway* (1942), William Wyler's *The Memphis Belle* (1944), and John Huston's *The Battle of San Pietro* (1944). The last three were shot on location and were made especially effective by their immediacy.

When World War II ended, the American film industry seemed to be in an ideal position. Full-scale mobilization had ended the Depression domestically, and victory had opened vast, unchallenged markets in the war-torn economies of western Europe and Japan. Furthermore, from 1942 through 1945, Hollywood had experienced the most stable and lucrative three years in its history, and in 1946, when two-thirds of the American population went to the movies at least once a week, the studios earned record-breaking profits. The euphoria ended quickly, however, as inflation and labour unrest boosted domestic production costs and as important foreign markets, including Britain and Italy, were temporarily lost to protectionist quotas.

The industry was more severely weakened in 1948, when a federal antitrust suit against the five major and three minor studios ended in the "Paramount decrees," which forced the studios to divest themselves of their theatre chains and mandated competition in the exhibition sector for the first time in 30 years. Finally, the advent of network television broadcasting in the 1940s provided Hollywood with its first real competition for American leisure time by offering consumers "movies in the home."

The American film industry's various problems and the nation's general postwar disillusionment generated several new film types in the late 1940s. Although the studios continued to produce traditional genre films, such as westerns and musicals, their financial difficulties encouraged them to make realistic small-scale dramas rather than fantastic lavish epics, the new lower-budget films tried to develop thought-provoking or perverse stories reflecting the psychological and social problems besetting returning war veterans and others adapting to postwar life. Some of the American cinema's grimmest and most naturalistic films were produced during this period, including those of the so-called social consciousness cycle, which attempted to deal realistically with such endemic problems as racism (Elia Kazan's *Gentleman's Agreement*, 1947; Alfred Werker's *Lost Boundaries*, 1949), alcoholism (Stuart Heisler's *Smash-Up*, 1947), and mental illness (Anatole Litvak's *The Snake Pit*, 1948); the semidocumentary melodrama, which reconstructed true criminal cases and was often shot on location (Kazan's *Boomerang*, 1947; Henry Hathaway's *Kiss of Death*, 1947); and the film noir, whose dark, fatalistic interpretations of contemporary American reality are unique in the industry's history (Tay Garnett's *The Postman Always Rings Twice*, 1946; Orson Welles's *The Lady from Shanghai*, 1947; Jacques Tourneur's *Out of the Past*, 1947; Abraham Polonsky's *Force of Evil*, 1948).

THE FEAR OF COMMUNISM

Film content was influenced strongly by the fear of communism that pervaded the United States during the late 1940s and early '50s. Anticommunist "witch-hunts" began in Hollywood in 1947 when the House Un-American Activities Committee (HUAC) decided to investigate communist influence in motion pictures. More than 100 witnesses, including many of Hollywood's most talented and popular artists, were called before the committee to answer questions about their own and their associates' alleged communist affiliations. On Nov. 24, 1947, a group of

eight screenwriters and two directors, later known as the Hollywood Ten, were sentenced to serve up to a year in prison for refusing to testify. That evening the members of the Association of Motion Picture Producers, which included the leading studio heads, published what became known as the Waldorf Declaration, in which they fired the members of the Hollywood Ten and expressed their support of HUAC. The studios, afraid to antagonize already shrinking audiences, then initiated an unofficial policy of blacklisting, refusing to employ any person even suspected of having communist associations. Hundreds of people were fired from the industry, and many creative artists were never able to work in Hollywood again. Throughout the blacklisting era, filmmakers refrained from making any but the most conservative motion pictures; controversial topics or new ideas were carefully avoided. The resulting creative stagnation, combined with financial difficulties, contributed significantly to the demise of the studio system, although, paradoxically, the actions that the studios took between 1952 and 1965, including the practice of blacklisting, can be viewed as an attempt to halt the industry's decline.

THE THREAT OF TELEVISION

The film industry believed that the greatest threat to its continued success was posed by television, especially in light of the Paramount decrees. The studios seemed to be losing their control of the nation's theatres at the same time that exhibitors were losing their audiences to television.

The studios therefore attempted to diminish television's appeal by exploiting the two obvious advantages that film enjoyed over the new medium—the size of its images and, at a time when all television broadcasting was in black and white, the ability to produce photographic colour. (In the 1952–53 season, the ability to produce multiple-track stereophonic sound joined this list.) In the late 1940s, fewer than 12 percent of Hollywood features were produced in colour, primarily because of the expense of three-strip Technicolor filming. In 1950, however, a federal consent decree dissolved the Technicolor Corporation's de facto monopoly on the process, and Kodak simultaneously introduced a new multilayered film stock in which emulsions sensitive to the red, green, and blue parts of the spectrum were bonded together on a single roll. Patented as Eastmancolor, this "integral tri-pack" process offered excellent colour resolution at a low cost because it could be used with conventional cameras. Its availability hastened the industry's conversion to full colour production. By 1954 more than 50 percent of American features were made in colour, and the figure reached 94 percent by 1970.

The aspect ratio (the ratio of width to height) of the projected motion-picture image had been standardized at 1.33 to 1 since 1932, but, as television eroded the film industry's domestic audience, the studios increased screen size as a way of attracting audiences back into theatres. For both optical and architectural reasons this change in size usually meant increased width, not increased height. Early experiments with multiple-camera wide-screen (Cinerama, 1952) and stereoscopic 3-D (Natural Vision, 1952) provoked audience interest, but it was an anamorphic process called CinemaScope that prompted the wide-screen revolution. Introduced by Twentieth Century–Fox in the biblical epic *The Robe* (1953), CinemaScope used an anamorphic lens to squeeze a wide-angle image onto conventional 35-mm film stock and a similar lens to restore the image's original width in projection. CinemaScope's aspect ratio was 2.55 to 1, and the system had the great advantage of requiring no special cameras, film stock, or projectors. By the end of 1954, every Hollywood studio but Paramount had leased a version of the process from Fox (Paramount adopted a nonanamorphic process called VistaVision that exposed double-frame images by running film through special cameras and projectors horizontally rather than vertically), and many studios were experimenting with wide-gauge film systems (e.g., Todd-AO, 1955; Panavision-70, 1960) that required special equipment but eliminated the distortion inherent in the anamorphic process.

Like the coming of sound, the conversion to wide-screen formats produced an initial regression as filmmakers learned how to compose and edit their images for the new elongated frame. Sound had promoted the rise of aurally intensive genres such as the musical and the gangster film, and the wide-screen format similarly created a bias in favour of visually spectacular subjects and epic scale. The emergence of the three- to four-hour wide-screen "blockbuster" in such films as *War and Peace*, *Around the World in Eighty Days*, and *The Ten Commandments* in 1956 coincided with the era's affinity for safe and sanitized material. Given the political paranoia of the times, few subjects could be treated seriously, and the studios concentrated on presenting traditional genre fare—westerns, musicals, comedies, and blockbusters—suitable for wide-screen treatment. Only a director like Hitchcock, whose style was oblique and imagist, could prosper in such a climate. He produced his greatest work during the period, much of it in VistaVision (*Rear Window*, 1954; *The Man Who Knew Too Much*,

Grace Kelly and James Stewart in *Rear Window* (1954), directed by Alfred Hitchcock.

1956; *Vertigo*, 1958; *North by Northwest*, 1959; *Psycho*, 1960; *The Birds*, 1963).

In spite of the major film companies' elaborate strategies of defense, they continued to decline throughout the 1950s and '60s. Because they could no longer dominate the exhibition sector, they faced serious competition for the first time from independent and foreign filmmakers. "Runaway" productions (films made away from the studios, frequently abroad, to take advantage of lower costs) became common, and the Production Code was dissolved as a series of federal court decisions between 1952 and 1958 extended First Amendment protection to motion pictures. As their incomes shrank, the major companies' vast studios and backlots became liabilities that ultimately crippled them. The minor companies, however, owned modest studio facilities and had lost nothing by the Paramount decrees because they controlled no theatres. They were thus able to prosper during this era, eventually becoming major companies themselves in the 1970s.

CINEMA IN ITALY

World War II physically and economically devastated the film industries of the Soviet Union, Japan, and most European nations. Italy's early surrender, however, left its facilities relatively intact, enabling the Italian cinema to lead the post-World War II film renaissance with its development of the Neorealist movement. Although it had roots in both Soviet expressive realism and French poetic realism, Neorealism was decidedly national in focus, taking as its subject the day-to-day reality of a country traumatized by political upheaval and war.

Most of the major figures in the Neorealist movement had studied at Benito Mussolini's national film school, the Centro Sperimentale di Cinematografia (founded 1935; "Experimental Centre of Cinematography"), but they vigorously rejected the stagy, artificial style associated with the *telefono bianco* films in favour of a Marxist aesthetic of everyday life. The first identifiable Neorealist film was Luchino Visconti's *Ossessione* (1942; *Obsession*), a bleak contemporary melodrama shot on location in the countryside around Ferrara. It was suppressed by the fascist censors, however, so international audiences were first introduced to the movement through Roberto Rossellini's *Roma, città aperta* (1945; *Open City*), which was shot on location in the streets of Rome only two months after Italy's surrender. The film featured both professional and nonprofessional actors and focused on ordinary people caught up in contemporary events. Its documentary texture, postrecorded sound track, and improvisational quality became the hallmark of the Neorealist movement. Rossellini followed it with *Paisà*

(1946; *Paisan*) and *Germania, anno zero* (1947; *Germany, Year Zero*) to complete his "war trilogy." Visconti's second contribution to Neorealism was *La terra trema* (1948; *The Earth Trembles*), an epic of peasant life that was shot on location in a Sicilian fishing village. In many respects it is more exemplary of the movement than *Ossessione*, and it is widely regarded as a masterpiece. Neorealism's third major director was Vittorio De Sica, who worked in close collaboration with scriptwriter Cesare Zavattini, the movement's major theorist and spokesman. De Sica's films sometimes tend toward sentimentality, but in *Sciuscià* (1946; *Shoeshine*), *Ladri di biciclette* (1948; *The Bicycle Thief*), and *Umberto D.* (1952), he produced works central to the movement.

Neorealism was the first postwar cinema to reject Hollywood's narrative conventions and studio production techniques, and, as such, it had enormous influence on future movements such as British Social Realism, Brazilian Cinema Nôvo, and French and Czech New Wave. It also heralded the practices of shooting on location using natural lighting and postsynchronizing sound that later became standard in the film industry. Despite its influence, in the 1950s Neorealism disappeared as a distinct national movement. Italian cinema nevertheless remained prominent through the films of several gifted directors who began their careers as

Neorealists and went on to produce their major work during the 1960s and '70s.

Federico Fellini had worked as a scriptwriter for Rossellini before directing in the 1950s an impressive series of films whose form was Neorealist but whose content was allegorical (*I vitelloni* [*The Loafers*], 1953; *La strada* [*The Road*], 1954; *Le notti di Cabiria* [*Nights of Cabiria*], 1956). During the 1960s

Scene from *Otto e mezzo* (1963; *8 1/2*), directed by Federico Fellini.

Fellini's work became increasingly surrealistic (*La dolce vita* [*The Sweet Life*], 1960; *Otto e mezzo* [*8½*], 1963; *Giulietta degli spiriti* [*Juliet of the Spirits*], 1965; *Fellini Satyricon*, 1969), and by the 1970s he was perceived to be a flamboyant ironic fantasist—a reputation that sustained him through such serious and successful films as *Fellini Roma* (1972), *Amarcord* (1974), and *E la nave va* (1983; *And the Ship Sails On*).

Michelangelo Antonioni had also collaborated with Rossellini. Accordingly, his first films were Neorealist documentary shorts (*Gente del Po* [*People of the Po*], 1947), but during the 1950s he turned increasingly to an examination of the Italian bourgeoisie in such films as *Cronaca di un amore* (1950; *Story of a Love Affair*), *La signora senza camelie* (1953; *Camille Without Camellias*), and *Le amiche* (1955; *The Girlfriends*), and in the early 1960s Antonioni produced a trilogy on the malaise of the middle class that made him internationally famous. In *L'avventura* (1959; *The Adventure*), *La notte* (1960; *The Night*), and *L'eclisse* (1962; *The Eclipse*), he used long-take sequence shots equating film time with real time to create a vision of the reverberating emptiness of modern urban life. Antonioni then began to use colour expressionistically in *Deserto rosso* (1964; *Red Desert*) and *Blow-Up* (1966) to convey alienation and abstraction from human feeling, and all of his later works in some way concerned the breakdown of personal relationships (*Zabriskie Point*, 1970; *Identificazione di una donna* [*Identification of a Woman*], 1982) and of identity itself (*Professione: Reporter* [*The Passenger*], 1975).

While Fellini and Antonioni were putting Italy in the vanguard of modernist cinema, the country's second post-World War II generation of directors emerged. Ermanno Olmi (*Il posto* [*The Job*], 1961; *Un certo giorno* [*One Fine Day*], 1968; L'albero degli zoccoli [*The Tree of Wooden Clogs*], 1979) continued the Neorealist tradition in his tales of ordinary people caught up in systems beyond their comprehension. Pier Paolo Pasolini, who had worked as a scriptwriter for Fellini, achieved international recognition for *Il vangelo secondo Matteo* (1964; *The Gospel According to St. Matthew*), a brilliant semidocumentary reconstruction of the life of Christ with Marxist overtones. Pasolini went on to direct a series of astonishing, often outrageous films that set forth a Marxist interpretation of history and myth—*Edipo re* (1967; *Oedipus Rex*), *Teorema* (1968; *Theorem*), *Porcile* (1969; *Pigsty*), *Medea* (1969), *Salò* (1975)—before his murder in 1975. Like Pasolini, Bernardo Bertolucci was a Marxist intellectual whose films attempt to correlate sexuality, ideology, and history; his most successful films were *Il conformista* (1970; *The Conformist*), a striking dissection of the psychopathology of fascism; *Ultimo tango a*

Parigi (1972; *Last Tango in Paris*), a meditation on sex and death; and *Novecento* (1976; *1900*), a six-hour epic covering 50 years of Italian class conflict. Other important Italian filmmakers include Francesco Rosi (*Salvatore Giuliano*, 1962), Marco Bellocchio (*La Cina è vicina* [*China Is Near*], 1967), Marco Ferreri (*La Grande Bouffe* [*Blow-Out*], 1973), Ettore Scola (*Una giornata speciale* [*A Special Day*], 1977), Paolo Taviani and Vittorio Taviani (*Padre padrone* [*Father and Master*], 1977), Franco Brusati (*Dimenticare Venezia* [*To Forget Venice*], 1979), and Lina Wertmüller (*Pasqualino settebellezze* [*Seven Beauties*], 1976).

Beginning in the 1970s, the declining European economy compelled many Italian directors to make coproductions with American, French, German, and Swedish companies. In order to maximize profits, several such films featured international stars in leading roles. This dependence on world markets—as well as the increased popularity of television throughout Italy—often led to the loss of national identity in Italian films, although such filmmakers as Roberto Benigni, Carlo Verdone, and Maurizio Nichetti were able to use the new situation to good advantage. Perhaps the most individual voice in Italian cinema during the 1990s was Nanni Moretti, whose humourous, satiric works, such as *Caro diario* (1994; *Dear Diary*), critique the social values of the late 20th century. Moretti's family drama *La stanza del figlio* (*The*

Son's Room) won the top award at the 2001 Cannes film festival.

CINEMA IN FRANCE

French cinema of the occupation and postwar era produced many fine films (Marcel Carné's *Les Enfants du paradis* [*The Children of Paradise*], 1945; Jean Cocteau's *La Belle et la bête* [*Beauty and the Beast*], 1946; René Clément's *Jeux interdits* [*Forbidden Games*], 1952; Jacques Becker's *Casque d'or* [*Golden Helmet*], 1952; Henri-Georges Clouzot's *Le Salaire de la peur* [*The Wages of Fear*], 1953), but their mode of presentation relied heavily on script and was predominantly literary. There were exceptions in the austere classicism of Robert Bresson (*Le Journal d'un curé de campagne* [*The Diary of a Country Priest*], 1950; *Un Condamné à mort s'est échappé* [*A Man Escaped*], 1956), the absurdist comedy of Jacques Tati (*Les Vacances de M. Hulot* [*Mr. Hulot's Holiday*], 1953; *Mon oncle* [*My Uncle*], 1958), and the lush, magnificently stylized masterworks of the German émigré Max Ophüls, whose *La Ronde* (1950), *Le Plaisir* (1952), *Madame de...* (1953), and *Lola Montès* (1955) represent significant contributions to world cinema. An independent documentary movement, which produced such landmark nonfiction films as Georges Rouquier's

Farrebique (1948), Georges Franju's *Le Sang des bêtes* (1949; *The Blood of the Beasts*), and Alain Resnais's *Nuit et brouillard* (1956; *Night and Fog*), also emerged at this time. It provided a training ground for young directors outside the traditional industry system and influenced the independent production style of the movement that culminated in the French postwar period of renewal—the Nouvelle Vague, or New Wave.

The most important source of the New Wave lay in the theoretical writings of Alexandre Astruc and, more prominently, of André Bazin, whose thought molded an entire generation of filmmakers, critics, and scholars. In 1948 Astruc formulated the concept of the *caméra-stylo* ("camera-pen"), in which film was regarded as a form of audiovisual language and the filmmaker, therefore, as a kind of writer in light. Bazin's influential journal *Cahiers du cinéma,* founded in 1951, elaborated this notion and became the headquarters of a group of young *cinéphiles* ("film lovers")—the critics François Truffaut, Jean-Luc Godard, Claude Chabrol, Jacques Rivette, and Eric Rohmer—who were to become the major directors of the New Wave. Bazin's basic principle was a rejection of montage aesthetics—both radical Eisensteinian cutting and Hollywood-style continuity, or invisible, editing—in favour of the long take and composition in depth, or what he called mise-en-scène. Borrowed from the theatre, this term literally means "the placing in the scene," but Bazin used it to designate such elements of filmic structure as camera placement and movement, the lighting of shots, and blocking of action—that is, everything that precedes the editing process.

The *Cahiers* critics embraced mise-en-scène aesthetics and borrowed the idea of authorship from Astruc. In proposing *la politique des auteurs* ("the policy of authors"), christened the auteur theory by the American critic Andrew Sarris, they maintained that film should be a medium of personal artistic expression and that the best films are those imprinted with their makers' individual signature. As a logical consequence of this premise, the *Cahiers* critics rejected mainstream French cinema and its "tradition of quality" in favour of the classic mise-en-scène tradition (exemplified in the films of Louis Feuillade, F.W. Murnau, Erich von Stroheim, Renoir, Welles, and Ophüls), the films of Hollywood studio directors who had transcended the constraints of the system to make personal films (Howard Hawks, Josef von Sternberg, Hitchcock, and Ford), and the low-budget American B movie in which the director usually had total control over production.

The first films of the New Wave were independently produced dramatic shorts shot in 16-mm by the *Cahiers* critics in 1956–57, but 1959 was the year that brought the movement to international prominence, when each of its three major figures made their first features. Truffaut's *Les Quatre Cents Coups* (*The 400 Blows*), Resnais's *Hiroshima, mon amour*, and Godard's *À bout de souffle* (*Breathless*) were all in their different ways paradigms of a fresh new style based on elliptical editing and location shooting with handheld cameras. This style was both radically destructive of classic Hollywood continuity and pragmatically suited to the New Wave's need to make its films quickly and cheaply. Its ultimate effect was to deconstruct the narrative language that had evolved over the previous 60 years and to create a reflexive cinema, or meta-cinema, whose techniques provided a continuous comment on its own making.

The critical and commercial success of the first New Wave features produced an unprecedented creative explosion within the French industry. Between 1960 and 1964, literally hundreds of low-budget, stylistically experimental films were made by cinéphiles with little or no experience. Many of these ended in failure, and the New Wave as a collective phenomenon was over by 1965. But the three figures who had initiated the movement, and a small group of sophisticated and talented filmmakers—Chabrol, Rivette, Rohmer, Louis Malle, Agnès Varda, and Jacques Demy—dominated French cinema until well into the 1970s, and several continued to make significant contributions into the next century.

François Truffaut was the most commercially successful of the original New Wave group, and, through such films as *Jules et Jim* (1961) and the autobiographical "Antoine Doinel" series, which began with *Les Quatre Cents Coups,* he acquired a reputation as a romantic ironist. Truffaut's range also extended to parodies of Hollywood genres (*Tirez sur le pianiste* [*Shoot the Piano Player*], 1960), homages to Hitchcock (*La Mariée était en noir* [*The Bride Wore Black*], 1967), historical reconstructions (*L'Enfant sauvage* [*The Wild Child*], 1970), reflexive narratives (*La Nuit américaine* [*Day for Night*], 1973), and literary adaptations (*L'Histoire d'Adèle H.* [*The Story of Adele H.*], 1975; *Le Dernier Métro* [*The Last Metro*], 1980).

Jean-Luc Godard was the most stylistically and politically radical of the early New Wave directors. Some of his early films were parodies of Hollywood genres (*Une Femme est une femme* [*A Woman Is a Woman*], 1961; *Alphaville,* 1965; *Pierrot le fou,* 1965), but the majority of them treated political and social themes from a Marxist, and finally Maoist, perspective (*Le Petit Soldat* [*The Little Soldier*], 1960; *Vivre sa vie* [*My Life to Live*], 1962; *Les Carabiniers* [*The Riflemen*], 1963; *Bande à part* [*Band of Outsiders*], 1964; *Une Femme mariée* [*A Married Woman*],

Jean-Pierre Léaud and Anne Wiazemsky in *La Chinoise* (1967), directed by Jean-Luc Godard.

1964). With *Masculin féminin* (1966), Godard turned from narrative to cinema verité-style essay, and his later films became increasingly ideological and structurally random (*Made in U.S.A.*, 1966; *Deux ou trois choses que je sais d'elle* [*Two or Three Things I Know About Her*], 1967; *La Chinoise*, 1967; *Week-end*, 1967; *One Plus One* [also called *Sympathy for the Devil*], 1968). During the 1970s, Godard made films for the radical Dziga Vertov production collective (*Pravda*, 1969; *Le Vent d'est* [*Wind from the East*], 1969; *Letter to Jane*, 1972) and experimented with combinations of film and videotape (*Numéro deux* [*Number Two*], 1975; *La Communication*, 1976). In the 1980s Godard returned to theatrical filmmaking, purified of ideology but no less controversial for it, with such provocative features as *Sauve qui peut (la vie)* (1980; *Every Man for Himself*), *Passion* (1982), *Je vous salue, Marie* (1986; *Hail Mary*), and *Éloge de l'amour* (2001; *In Praise of Love*).

Alain Resnais was slightly older than the *Cahiers* group, but he identified with the New Wave through style and theme. His most famous film is the postmodern mystery *L'Année dernière à Marienbad* (1961; *Last Year at Marienbad*), which questions the processes of thought and memory—central concerns in Resnais's work. *Muriel* (1963), *La Guerre est finie* (1966; *The War Is Over*), *Stavisky* (1974), *Providence* (1977), and *Mon oncle d'Amérique*

(1978; *My American Uncle*) are all in various ways concerned with the effects of time on human memory from both a historical and a personal perspective.

Other important New Wave figures with lasting influence are Claude Chabrol, whose entire career can be seen as an extended homage to Hitchcock; Louis Malle, a master of film types who relocated to the United States; Eric Rohmer, whose "moral tales," including *Ma nuit chez Maud* (1968; *My Night at Maud's*) and *Le Genou de Claire* (1970; *Claire's Knee*), established the ironic perspective on human passion that he maintained in later films; Agnès Varda, famed for her improvisational style; Jacques Demy, whose best films are homages to the Hollywood musical; and Jacques Rivette, the most austerely abstract and experimental of the *Cahiers* group.

Few national movements have influenced international cinema as strongly as the French New Wave. By promoting the concept of personal authorship, its directors demonstrated that film is an audiovisual language that can be crafted into "novels" and "essays"; and, by deconstructing classic Hollywood conventions, they added dimensions to this language that made it capable of expressing a new range of internal and external states. In the process, the New Wave helped to reinvigorate the stylistically moribund cinemas then found in

Britain, West Germany, and the United States; it created a current of "second waves" and "third waves" in the already flourishing Italian, Polish, Czech, Hungarian, and Japanese cinemas.

The New Wave made France the leading centre of Modernist and postmodern film and film theory, a position it continued to hold for many years. By the 1990s France had followed the lead of other European countries in assimilating into the world market. The influence of the New Wave was still evident, but increased demands for commercial fare resulted in several crime thrillers and period costume dramas, genres that were often specialties of young directors.

Unique among European filmmakers, however, many French directors remained unfettered by commercial demands. At the turn of the 21st century, Chabrol was still a dominant force, with films such as *La Cérémonie* (1995; *Judgment in Stone*) demonstrating his continued mastery of the psychological thriller. Prominent young directors included Manuel Poirier, who specialized in affectionate, offbeat romances and "buddy pictures," such as *Western* (1997); Claire Simon, who, after several years of directing documentaries, adapted her characteristic ironic humour to such fiction films as *Sinon, oui* (1997; *A Foreign Body*) and *Ça c'est vraiment toi* (2000; *That's Just like You*);

and Robert Guédiguian, a writer-producer-director known for works such as *Marius et Jeannette* (1997) and *Á la place du coeur* (1998), which effectively blend affectionate character studies with biting social satire.

CINEMA IN GREAT BRITAIN

In Great Britain the post-World War II cinema was even more literary than in France, relying heavily on the adaptation of classics in the work of such directors as Laurence Olivier (*Henry V*, 1944; *Hamlet*, 1948; *Richard III*, 1955), David Lean (*Great Expectations*, 1946; *Oliver Twist*, 1948), and Anthony Asquith (*The Importance of Being Earnest*, 1952). Even less-conventional films had literary sources (Carol Reed's *Outcast of the Islands*, 1951; Michael Powell and Emeric Pressberger's *The Red Shoes*, 1948, and *The Tales of Hoffman*, 1951). There were exceptions to this trend in a series of witty, irreverent comedies made for Michael Balcon's Ealing Studios (*Kind Hearts and Coronets*, 1949; *The Lavender Hill Mob*, 1951; *The Man in the White Suit*, 1951), most of them starring Alec Guinness, but, on the whole, British postwar cinema was elitist and culturally conservative.

In reaction, a younger generation of filmmakers led by Lindsay Anderson,

Czechoslovak-born Karel Reisz, and Tony Richardson organized the Free Cinema movement in the mid-1950s. Its purpose was to produce short low-budget documentaries illuminating problems of contemporary life (Anderson's *O Dreamland*, 1953; Richardson's *Momma Don't Allow*, 1955). Grounded in the ideology and practice of Neorealism, Free Cinema emerged simultaneously with a larger social movement assailing the British class structure and calling for the replacement of bourgeois elitism with liberal working-class values. In the cinema this antiestablishment agitation resulted in the New Cinema, or Social Realist, movement signaled by Reisz's *Saturday Night and Sunday Morning* (1960), the first British postwar feature with a working-class protagonist and proletarian themes. Stylistically influenced by the New Wave, with which it was concurrent, the Social Realist film was generally shot in black and white on location in the industrial Midlands and cast with unknown young actors and actresses. Like the New Wave films, Social Realist films were independently produced on low budgets (many of them for Woodfall Film Productions, the company founded in 1958 by Richardson and playwright John Osborne, one of the principal Angry Young Men, to adapt the latter's *Look Back in Anger*), but their freshness of both content and form attracted an international audience. Some of the most

Albert Finney in *Tom Jones* (1963), directed by Tony Richardson.

famous were Richardson's *A Taste of Honey* (1961) and *The Loneliness of the Long Distance Runner* (1962), John Schlesinger's *A Kind of Loving* (1962) and *Billy Liar* (1963), Anderson's *This Sporting Life* (1963), and Reisz's *Morgan: A Suitable Case for Treatment* (1966).

These films and others like them brought such prestige to the British film industry that London briefly became the production capital of the Western world, delivering such homegrown international hits as Richardson's *Tom Jones* (1963), Schlesinger's *Darling* (1965), Richard Lester's two Beatles films, *A Hard Day's Night* (1964) and *Help!* (1965), Schlesinger's *Far from the Madding Crowd* (1967), and Anderson's *If...* (1968), as well as such foreign importations as Roman Polanski's *Repulsion* (1965) and *Cul-de-sac* (1966), Truffaut's *Fahrenheit 451* (1966), Antonioni's *Blow-Up*

Stanley Kubrick (*foreground*) directing a scene from *2001: A Space Odyssey* (1968).

(1966), and American Stanley Kubrick's *2001: A Space Odyssey* (1968) and *A Clockwork Orange* (1971). This activity inspired a new, more visually oriented generation of British filmmakers—Peter Yates, John Boorman, Ken Russell, Nicolas Roeg, and Ridley Scott—who would make their mark in the 1970s; but, as England's economy began its precipitous decline during that decade, so too did its film industry. Many British directors and performers defected to Hollywood, while the English-language film market simultaneously experienced a vigorous and unprecedented challenge from Australia. In the 1980s, amid widespread speculation about the collapse of the film industry, British annual production reached an all-time low.

Great Britain's film industry, however, has a long history of rebounding from periods of crisis. A major factor in the revival of British cinema during the late 20th century was the founding in 1982 of Channel 4, a television network devoted to commissioning—rather than merely producing—original films. Its success led to the establishment of a subsidiary, FilmFour Ltd., in 1998. Internationally acclaimed films produced or coproduced under either the Channel 4 or the FilmFour banner include *A Room with a View* (1986), *The Crying Game* (1992), *Four Weddings and a Funeral* (1994), *Trainspotting* (1996), *Secrets and Lies* (1996), *The Full Monty* (1997), and *Welcome to Sarajevo* (1997). Also contributing to the resurgence of British film was the National Lottery, which, after its establishment in 1994, annually contributed millions of pounds to the film industry.

CINEMA IN GERMANY

Germany's catastrophic defeat in World War II and the subsequent partitioning of the country virtually destroyed its film industry, which had already been corrupted by the Nazis. Rebuilt during the 1950s, the West German industry became the fifth largest producer in the world, but the majority of its output consisted of low-quality *Heimatfilme* ("homeland films") for the domestic market. When this market collapsed in the 1960s because of changing demographic patterns and the diffusion of television, the industry was forced to turn to the federal government for subsidies. In recognition of the crisis, 26 writers and filmmakers at the Oberhausen film festival in 1962 drafted a manifesto proclaiming the death of German cinema and demanding the establishment of a *junger deutscher Film*, a "young German cinema." The members of this Oberhausen group became the founders of Das Neue Kino, or the New German Cinema, which was brought into being over the next decade through the establishment of the Kuratorium Junger Deutscher Film (1965; Young German Film Board, a grant agency with funding drawn from the cultural budgets of the federal states), the Filmförderungsanstalt, or FFA (Film Subsidies Board, which generated production funds by levying a federal tax in part on theatre tickets), and the independent distributing company Filmverlag der Autoren (1971; Authors' Film-Publishing Group), with additional funding from the two West German television networks.

These institutions made it possible for a new generation of German filmmakers to produce their first features and established a vital new cinema for West Germany that attempted to examine the nation's *unbewältige Vergangenheit*, or "unassimilated past." The first such films, which were deeply influenced by the New Wave, especially by the work of Godard, included Volker Schlöndorff's *Der junge Törless* (1966; *Young Torless*) and Alexander Kluge's *Die Artisten in der Zirkuskuppel: ratlos* (1968; *The Artists Under the Big Top: Disoriented*). In the 1970s, however, three major figures emerged as leaders of the movement—Rainer Werner Fassbinder, Werner Herzog, and Wim Wenders.

Fassbinder was the most prolific, having made more than 40 features before he died in 1982. His films are also the most flamboyant. Nearly all of them take the form of extreme melodrama, ending in murder or suicide—*Warum läuft Herr R. amok?* (1969; *Why Does Herr R. Run Amok?*), *Die bitteren Tränen der Petra von Kant* (1972; *The Bitter Tears of Petra von Kant*), and *Angst essen Seele auf* (1973; *Ali: Fear Eats the Soul*)—and several are consciously focused on German wartime and postwar society (*Die Ehe der Maria Braun* [*The Marriage of Maria Braun*], 1979; *Lola*, 1981; *Veronika Voss*, 1982).

Herzog's films tended more toward the mystical and the spiritual than the social, although there is nearly always some contemporary referent in his work—the image of idealism turned to barbarism in *Aguirre, der Zorn Gottes* (1972; *Aguirre, the Wrath of God*); the hopeless inability of science to address the human condition in *Jeder für sich und Gott gegen alle* (1974; *Every Man for Himself and God Against All*, or *The Enigma of Kaspar Hauser*); the inherently destructive nature of technology in *Herz aus Glas* (1977; *Heart of Glass*); the incomprehensible nature of pestilence in his remake of Murnau's *Nosferatu* (1979).

Wenders, on the other hand, was profoundly postmodern in his contemplation of alienation through spatial metaphor. In such works of existential questing as *Die Angst des Tormanns beim Elfmeter* (1971; *The Goalie's Anxiety at the Penalty Kick*) and *Im Lauf der Zeit* (1976; "In the Course of Time"; *Kings of the Road*), he addressed the universal phenomena of dislocation and rootlessness that afflict modern society.

The state subsidy system enabled hundreds of filmmakers, including many women (e.g., Margarethe von Trotta) and minorities, to participate in the New German Cinema. With the exception of the work of Fassbinder, Herzog, and Wenders, however, the New German Cinema did not find a large audience outside West Germany. Yet in terms of exploring and extending the audio-language system of film, it was to the

1970s and '80s very much what the New Wave was to the '60s, and its influence was widely felt.

By the reunification of Germany in 1990, a national identity had still not been forged in any of the various arts. Several outstanding German directors and production artists did emerge, but most of them achieved their greatest success in Hollywood. Roland Emmerich (*Independence Day,* 1996; *The Patriot,* 2000) proved to be a skillful practitioner of the action-adventure genre, and Wolfgang Petersen, who received international acclaim for *Das Boot* (1982), earned a reputation for tense thrillers (*In the Line of Fire,* 1993) and unrelenting visual spectacles (*The Perfect Storm,* 2000). German cinematographers (Michael Ballhaus, Karl Walter Lindenlaub) and composers (Hans Zimmer, Christopher Franke) were also among the more notable artisans working in Hollywood films at the turn of the 21st century.

CINEMA IN AFRICA

The development of an indigenous film culture in Africa occurred at different moments in the history of the continent. The various timelines are related to the political, social, and economic situations in each country and to the varying effects of colonialism on the continent. Only Egypt had a truly active film industry for the first half of the 20th century;

the development of cinema elsewhere on the continent was largely the result of individual efforts. One such example is Paul Soumanou Vieyra, the first African graduate of the French film school Institut des Hautes Études Ciné, who joined with friends to produce the short film *Afrique sur Seine* (1955), considered the first fiction film by black Africans.

Some countries, such as Morocco, did not develop a strong national cinema; others, such as Algeria and Tunisia, nationalized all or parts of their film industries. Several African nations joined the Fédération Pan-Africaine des Cinéastes (FEPACI; "Federation of Pan-African Filmmakers"), formed in 1969 to oversee the political and financial problems of the film industries throughout the continent.

As the 20th century drew to a close, many filmmakers and scholars began to examine the questions of, first, what constitutes an "African film" and, second, how film can best deal with the diaspora of the African people. On one hand, African filmmakers had to acknowledge and learn from the conventions of Western film. On the other, they wanted to highlight and preserve aspects of African culture that had been threatened by Western colonialism. As part of this search to define the goals of African cinema, African filmmakers often used the medium to explore the social issues plaguing postcolonial Africa. Directors such as Adama Drabo (*Ta Dona* [*Fire*], 1991) and Moufida Tlatli (*Les Silences du palais* [*The Silences of the Palace*], 1994) explored such matters as education, the environment, and women's rights and suggested that traditional approaches to such issues had to be adapted to the realities of contemporary Africa. Aspects of these realities were examined by such directors as Tsitsi Dangarembga (*Everyone's Child*, 1996) and Salem Mekuria (*Ye Wonz Maibel* [*Deluge*], 1995), who dealt with the AIDS crisis and political violence, respectively. Colonization itself was examined by such directors as Bassek ba Kobhio, whose satiric study of Albert Schweitzer, *Le Grand Blanc de Lambaréné* (1995; *The Great White Man of Lambaréné*), shows how colonialism damaged both the colonizer and the colonized.

CINEMA IN JAPAN

Although more than half of Japan's theatres were destroyed by U.S. bombing during World War II, most of its studio facilities were left intact. Japan, therefore, continued to produce films in quantity during the Allied occupation (1945–52). Many traditional Japanese subjects were forbidden by the Allied Command as promoting feudalism, however, including all films classified as *jidai-geki* ("period dramas"). Nevertheless, the film that first brought Japanese cinema to international attention belonged

A scene from *Kagemusha* (1980), directed by Kurosawa Akira.

to that category: Kurosawa Akira's *Rashomon* (1950), which won the Golden Lion at the 1951 Venice film festival. The film, a meditation on the nature of truth set in the medieval past, marked the beginning of the Japanese cinema's unprecedented renaissance. During this period, new export markets opened in the West, and Japanese filmmakers produced some of their finest work, winning festival awards throughout the world. Kurosawa, who was already well known in his homeland for a number of wartime and postwar genre films, became the most famous Japanese director in the West on the strength of his masterful samurai epics—*Shichinin no samurai* (1954; *Seven Samurai*), *Kumonosu-jo* (1957; *Throne of Blood*), *Kakushi toride no san akunin* (1958; *The Hidden Fortress*), *Yojimbo* (1961), and *Sanjuro* (1962)—which raised the chambara, or "sword-fight," film to the status of art. He made films in other genres, including literary adaptations, *gendai-geki* ("modern dramas"), gangster films, and period films that cannot be categorized at all (*Akahige* [*Red Beard*], 1965; *Dersu Uzala*, 1975); but Kurosawa always returned to the samurai form for his most profound statements about life and art (*Kagemusha* [*The Shadow Warrior*], 1980; *Ran*, 1985).

Two other established directors who produced their greatest films in the postwar period were Mizoguchi Kenji and Ozu Yasujirō. Both had begun their careers in the silent era and were more traditionally Japanese in style and content than Kurosawa. Mizoguchi's films, whether period (*Sansho dayu* [*Sansho the Bailiff*], 1954) or contemporary (*Yoru no onnatachi* [*Women of the Night*], 1948), were frequently critiques of feudalism that focused on the condition of women within the social order. His greatest postwar films were *Saikaku ichidai onna* (1952; *The Life of Oharu*), the biography of a 17th-century courtesan, and *Ugetsu* (1953), the story of two men who abandon their wives for fame and glory during the 16th-century civil wars. Both were masterworks that clearly demonstrated Mizoguchi's expressive use of luminous decor, extended long takes, and deep-focus composition. As one of the great mise-en-scène directors, Mizoguchi can be compared to Murnau, Ophüls, and Welles, but his transcendental visual style makes him unique in the history of cinema.

Ozu Yasujirō too was a stylist, but the majority of his 54 films were *shomin-geki*, a variety of *gendai* film dealing with the lives of lower-middle-class families (*Tokyo monogatari* [*Tokyo Story*], 1953; *Higanbana* [*Equinox Flower*], 1958; *Ukigusa* [*Floating Weeds*], 1959). They were all very much alike and, in a sense, were all part of a single large film whose subject was the ordinary lives of ordinary people and the sacred beauty therein. Ozu's minimalist style—originating in both Zen

Buddhist aesthetics and the fact that most of his films were shot within the confines of a typical Japanese house—was based on his use of low-angle long takes in which the camera is positioned about three feet (one metre) off the floor at the eye level of a person seated on a tatami mat. This practice led Ozu to an especially imaginative use of offscreen space and "empty scenes."

The second postwar generation of Japanese filmmakers was mainly composed of Kobayashi Masaki, Ichikawa Kon, and Shindo Kaneto. Kobayashi is best known for *Ningen no joken* (1959–61; *The Human Condition*), his three-part antiwar epic set during Japan's brutal occupation of Manchuria, and the beautiful ghost film *Kwaidan* (1964). Ichikawa's major works were the pacifist films *Biruma no tategoto* (1956; *The Burmese Harp*) and *Nobi* (1959; *Fires on the Plain*). Shindo is best known for his poetic semidocumentary *Hadaka no shima* (1960; *The Island*) and the bizarre, folkloristic *Onibaba* (1964).

The third generation of postwar directors was most active during the 1960s and '70s. The group was deeply influenced by the French New Wave and included Teshigahara Hiroshi (*Suna no onna* [*Woman in the Dunes*], 1964), Masumura Yasuzo (*Akai Tenshi* [*The Red Angel*], 1965), Imamura Shohei (*Jinruigako nyumon* [*The Pornographers*], 1966), and Oshima Nagisa (*Ai no corrida* [*In the Realm of the Senses*], 1976). In the mid-1960s, however, competition from multiple-channel colour television and from American distributors forced the Japanese film industry into economic decline. A decade later, two major studios were bankrupt, and film production was increasingly dominated by two domestic exploitation genres: the *yakuza-eiga*, or contemporary urban gangster film, and the semipornographic *eroducti* on film. During the 1980s and '90s, Japan continued to produce the highest annual volume of films of any country in the world, but the studios remained in decline, and most serious productions, such as Kurosawa's *Kagemusha*, were funded by foreign interests. At the turn of the 21st century, funding for films remained low, although the market for films was the greatest ever. This situation led to the mass production of low-budget films, as well as to the increased popularity of amateur and experimental films.

CINEMA IN CHINA, TAIWAN, AND KOREA

Other Asian nations have had spotty cinematic histories, although most developed strong traditions during the late 20th century. The film industries of China, Taiwan, and Korea were marked by government restrictions for most of the 20th century, and the majority of their output consisted of propaganda films. The loosening of many restrictions in the 1980s and '90s resulted in a new wave of Asian directors who attained worldwide prominence. At the turn of the 21st century, China's "Fifth Generation Cinema" was known for such outstanding young directors as Zhang Yimou, who specialized in tales of political oppression and sexual repression. Korea's cinematic history is difficult to assess, because virtually

Zhang Ziyi (*left*) and Chang Chen in *Crouching Tiger, Hidden Dragon* (2000), directed by Ang Lee.

no films made prior to World War II exist, but works produced during the 1950s and '60s—the "golden age" of Korean cinema—gained a strong international reputation. The most successful Taiwanese directors of the late 20th century were Ang Lee, who directed films ranging from American morality tales such as *The Ice Storm* (1997) to the lavish martial-arts fantasy *Wo hu zang long* (2000; *Crouching Tiger, Hidden Dragon*); and Hou Hsiao-hsien, who was best known for his sensitive family dramas (*Hao nan hao nu* [*Good Men, Good Women*], 1995).

CINEMA IN INDIA

Serious postwar Indian cinema was for years associated with the work of Satyajit Ray, a director of singular talent who produced the great Apu trilogy (*Pather panchali* [*The Song of the Road*], 1955; *Aparajito* [*The Unvanquished*], 1956; *Apur sansar* [*The World of Apu*], 1959) under the influence of both Jean Renoir and Italian Neorealism. Ray continued to dominate Indian cinema through the 1960s and '70s with such artful Bengali films as *Devi* (1960; *The Goddess*), *Charulata* (1964; *The Lonely Wife*), *Aranyer din ratri* (1970; *Days and Nights in the Forest*), and *Ashani sanket* (1973; *Distant Thunder*). The Marxist intellectual Ritwik Ghatak received much less critical attention than his contemporary Ray, but through such films as *Ajantrik* (1958; *Pathetic Fallacy*) he created a body of alternative cinema that greatly influenced the rising generation.

In 1961 the Indian government established the Film Institute of India to train aspiring directors. It also formed the Film Finance Commission (FFC) to help fund independent production (and, later, experimental films). The National Film Archive was founded in 1964. These organizations encouraged the production of such important first features as Mrinal Sen's *Bhuvan Shome* (1969; *Mr. Shome*), Basu Chatterji's *Sara akaash* (1979; *The Whole Sky*), Mani Kaul's *Uski roti* (1969; *Daily Bread*), Kumar Shahani's *Maya darpan* (1972; *Mirror of Illusion*), Avtar Kaul's *27 Down* (1973), and M.S. Sathyu's *Garam hawa* (1973; *Scorching Wind*) and promoted the development of a nonstar "parallel cinema" centred in Bombay (Mumbai). A more traditional path was followed by Shyam Benegal, whose films (*Ankur* [*The Seedling*], 1974; *Nishant* [*Night's End*], 1975; *Manthan* [*The Churning*], 1976) are relatively realistic in form and deeply committed in sociopolitical terms. During the 1970s the regional industries of the southwestern states—especially those of Kerala and Karnataka—began to subsidize independent production, resulting in a "southern new wave" in the films of such diverse figures as G. Aravindan (*Kanchana sita* [*Golden Sita*], 1977), Adoor

Gopalakrishnan (*Elipathayam* [*Rat-Trap*], 1981), and Girish Karnad (*Kaadu* [*The Forest*], 1973). Despite the international recognition of these films, the Indian government's efforts to raise the artistic level of the nation's cinema were largely unsuccessful. During the 1970s, India was a land of more than one billion people, many of them illiterate and poor, whose exclusive access to audiovisual entertainment was film; television was the medium of the rich and powerful middle class. The Indian film industry was for much of the later 20th century the world's largest producer of low-quality films for domestic consumption, releasing on average 700 features per year in 16 languages.

CINEMA IN AUSTRALIA

Australia was a country virtually without a film industry until the late 1960s and early '70s, when the federal government established the Australian Film Development Corporation (after 1975, the Australian Film Commission) to subsidize the growth of an authentic national cinema, founded a national film school (the Australian Film and Television School, later the Australian Film Television and Radio School, or AFTRS) to train directors and other creative personnel, and initiated a system of lucrative tax incentives to attract foreign investment capital to the new industry. The result was a creative explosion unprecedented in the English-language cinema. Australia produced nearly 400 films between 1970 and 1985—more than had been made in all of its prior history.

With financing from the Film Commission and such semiofficial bodies as the New South Wales Film Corporation (by the end of the decade each of the federal states had its own funding agency), the first films began to appear in the early 1970s, and within the next few years several talented directors began to receive recognition, including Peter Weir (*Picnic at Hanging Rock*, 1975), Bruce Beresford (*The Getting of Wisdom*, 1977), Fred Schepisi (*The Chant of Jimmy Blacksmith*, 1978), George Miller (*Mad Max*, 1979), and the first AFTRS graduates, Phillip Noyce (*Newsfront*, 1978) and Gillian Armstrong (*My Brilliant Career*, 1979). Unlike the productions financed with foreign capital by the Canadian Film Development Corporation during the same period, these new Australian films had indigenous casts and crews and treated distinctly national themes. By the end of the 1970s, Australian motion pictures were being prominently featured at the Cannes international film festival and competing strongly at the box office in Europe. In 1981 Australia penetrated the American market with two critical hits, Beresford's *Breaker Morant* (1980) and Weir's *Gallipoli* (1981), and the following year it achieved a smashing commercial success with Miller's *Mad Max II*

(1981; retitled *The Road Warrior*, 1982). In the 1980s, many Australian directors worked for the American film industry, with varying degrees of success (Schepisi: *Barbarossa*, 1982; Beresford: *Tender Mercies*, 1983; Armstrong: *Mrs. Soffel*, 1984; Weir: *Witness*, 1985; Miller: *The Witches of Eastwick*, 1987). Despite this temporary talent drain and a decline in government tax concessions, the Australian cinema remained one of the most influential and creatively vital in the world. Prominent younger directors helped to maintain Australia's world status, including Baz Luhrmann, noted for his flamboyant visual style in such films as William Shakespeare's *Romeo + Juliet* (1996) and *Moulin Rouge* (2001), and P.J. Hogan, known for biting social comedies such as *Muriel's Wedding* (1994) and *My Best Friend's Wedding* (1997).

CINEMA IN RUSSIA, EASTERN EUROPE, AND CENTRAL ASIA

After World War II the Soviet Union's film industry experienced greater stagnation than that of any other nation except Germany. The Socialist Realism doctrine imposed during Stalin's dictatorship caused film production to fall from 19 features in 1945 to 5 in 1952. Although Stalin died the following year, the situation did not improve until the late 1950s, when such films as Mikhail Kalatozov's *Letyat zhuravli* (1957; *The Cranes Are Flying*) and Grigory Chukhrai's *Ballada o soldate* (1959; *Ballad of a Soldier*) emerged to take prizes at international film festivals. Some impressive literary adaptations were produced during the 1960s (Grigory Kozintsev's *Hamlet*, 1964; Sergey Bondarchuk's *Voyna i mir* [*War and Peace*], 1965–67), but the most important phenomenon of the decade was the graduation of a whole new generation of Soviet directors from the Vsesoyuzny Gosudarstvenny Institut Kinematografii (VGIK; "All-Union State Institute of Cinematography"), many of them from the non-Russian republics—the Ukraine (Yury Ilyenko, Larissa Shepitko), Georgia (Tengiz Abuladze, Georgy Danelia, Georgy Shengelaya and Eldar Shengelaya, Otar Yoseliani), Moldavia (Emil Lotyanu), Armenia (Sergey Paradzhanov), Lithuania (Vitautas Zhalekevichius), Kyrgyzstan (Bolotbek Shamshiev, Tolomush Okeyev), Uzbekistan (Elyor Ishmukhamedov, Ali Khamraev), Turkmenistan (Bulat Mansurov), and Kazakhstan (Abdulla Karsakbayev). By far the most brilliant of the new directors were Sergey Paradzhanov and Andrey Tarkovsky, who both were later persecuted for the unconventionality of their work. Paradzhanov's greatest film was *Tini zabutykh predkiv* (1964; *Shadows of Forgotten Ancestors*), a hallucinatory retelling of a Ukrainian folk legend of ravishing formal beauty. Tarkovsky created a body of work whose seriousness and symbolic resonance had a major impact on world cinema (*Andrey Rublev*, 1966; *Solaris*, 1971; *Zerkalo* [*Mirror*], 1974; *Stalker*, 1979; *Nostalghia* [*Nostalgia*], 1983), even though it was frequently tampered with by Soviet censors.

During the 1970s the policy of Socialist Realism (euphemized as "pedagogic realism") was again put into practice, so only two types of films could safely be made—literary adaptations and *bytovye*, or films of everyday life, such as Vladimir Menshov's *Moskva slezam ne verit* (1980; *Moscow Does Not Believe in Tears*). The Soviet cinema then experienced a far-reaching liberalization under the regime of Party Secretary Mikhail Gorbachev, whose policy of *glasnost* ("openness") took control of the industry away from bureaucratic censors and placed it in the hands of the filmmakers themselves. The Soviet cinema began to be revitalized as formerly suppressed films, such as Elem Klimov's *Agoniya* (1975), were distributed for the first time, and films that dealt confrontationally with Stalinism, such as Abuladze's *Pokayaniye* (1987; *Repentance*), were made without government interference.

Of the eastern European nations that fell under Soviet control after World War II, all except East Germany and Albania produced distinguished cinemas. Following the pattern set by the Soviets, these countries nationalized their film industries and established state film schools. They experienced a similar period of repressive government-imposed restrictions between 1945 and 1953, with a "thaw" during the late 1950s under Soviet premier Nikita Khrushchev. In Poland the loosening of ideological criteria gave rise to the so-called Polish school led by Jerzy Kawalerowicz (*Matka Joanna od aniołNw* [*Mother Joan of the Angels*], 1961), *Andrzej Munk* (Eroica, 1957), and, preeminently, Andrzej Wajda (*Pokolenie* [*A Generation*], 1954; *Kanał* [Canal], 1956; *Popiół i diament* [*Ashes and Diamonds*], 1958). Wajda's reputation grew throughout the 1960s and '70s, when he was joined by a second generation of Polish filmmakers that included Roman Polanski (*Nóż w wodzie* [*Knife in the Water*], 1962), Jerzy Skolimowski (*Bariera* [*Barrier*], 1966), and Krzysztof Zanussi (*Iluminacja* [*Illumination*], 1972). The Polish cinema expressed its support of the Solidarity trade union in the late 1970s through films by Wajda and such younger directors as Krysztof Kieślowski, Agnieszka Holland, and Feliks Falk.

The example of the Polish school encouraged the development of the Czech New Wave (1962–68), which became similarly entangled in politics. The Czechoslovak films that reached international audiences during this period were widely acclaimed for their freshness and formal experimentation, but they faced official disapproval at home, and many were suppressed for being politically subversive. Among the directors who were most critical of Pres. Antonín Novotný's hard-line regime were Věra Chytilová (*Sedmikrasky* [*Daisies*], 1966), Jaromil Jireš (*Zert* [*The Joke*], 1968), Ján Kadár (*Obchod na Korze* [*The Shop on Main Street*], 1965), Miloš Forman (*Hoří, má panenko* [*The Firemen's Ball*], 1967), Jirí Menzel (*Ostře sledované vlaky* [*Closely Watched Trains*], 1966),

Vaclav Neckar and Jitka Bendova in *Closely Watched Trains* (1966), directed by Jirí Menzel.

and Jan Němec (*O Slavnosti a hostech* [*The Party and the Guests*], 1966). When Alexander Dubček became president in January 1968, the Czechoslovak cinema eagerly participated in his brief attempt to give socialism "a human face." After the Soviet invasion of August 1968, many New Wave films were banned, the Czechoslovak film industry was reorganized, and several prominent figures, including Forman and Němec, were forced into exile.

In Hungary the abortive revolution of 1956 forestalled a postwar revival in film until the late 1960s, when the complex work of Miklós Jancsó (*Szegénylegények* [*The Round-Up*], 1965; *Csillagosok, katonák* [*The Red and the White*], 1967; *Még kér a nép* [*Red Psalm*], 1972) began to be internationally recognized. The rigorous training given students at the Budapest Film Academy ensured that the younger generation of Hungarian filmmakers would rise to prominence, as happened in the case of István Szabó (1981; *Mephisto*), István Gaál (*Magasiskola* [*Falcons*], 1970), Márta Mészáros (*Örökbefogadás* [*Adoption*], 1975), and Pál Gábor (1978; *Angi Vera*), many of whose films—as do Jancsó's—involve ideological interpretations of the national past.

Yugoslavia, Romania, and Bulgaria, unlike their more sophisticated Warsaw Pact allies, did not begin to develop film industries until after World War II. Yugoslavia was the most immediately successful and produced the countries' first internationally known director: the political avant-gardist Dušan Makavejev (*Ljubavni slucaj ili tragedija sluzbenice P.T.T.* [*The Tragedy of the Switchboard Operator*], 1967). Makavejev belonged to the late 1960s movement known as Novi Film (New Film), which also included such directors as Puriša Djordjević, Aleksandar Petrović, and Živojin Pavlović, all of whom were temporarily purged from the film industry during a reactionary period in the early 1970s. This dark period came to an end in 1976 when the filmmakers of the Prague school made their debuts. Goran Marković, Rajko Grlić, Srdjan Karanović, Lordan Zafranović, and Emir Kusturica were all graduates of the FAMU film school in Prague who had begun their careers working for Yugoslav television. Their offbeat, visually flamboyant social comedies brought a new breath of life into Yugoslav cinema and won a number of international prizes. Like Czechoslovakia, whose Jiří Trnka perfected puppet animation in the 1950s, Yugoslavia also became world famous for its animation, especially that of the "Zagreb school" founded by Vatroslav Mimica and Dušan Vukotić.

The Romanian and Bulgarian film industries did not begin to progress until the mid-1960s. Both countries subsequently developed authentic national cinemas and boasted directors well known on the festival circuit (e.g., the Romanians Dan Pița, Mircea Veroiu, and Mircea Daneliuc and the Bulgarians Hristo Hristov, Eduard Zakhariev, Georgi Dyulgerov, and award-winning animator Todor Dinov).

For decades, state money was readily available for filmmaking throughout the Soviet bloc countries, provided that the films were ideologically acceptable. This changed with the collapse of the Soviet Union in January 1992, whereupon funding became the chief obstacle to filmmaking in the region. By the late 1990s, fewer than two dozen films per year were produced in Russia. Adding to the decline were such factors as theatres that were closed or converted into businesses such as car dealerships, a home-video industry that was barely in its inceptive stages, and the popularity of American and Asian films. Although such directors as Sergey Bodrov and Vladimir Khotinenko received a degree of international acclaim, the financial situation of the film industries throughout Russia and eastern Europe during the 1990s suggested that it would be many years before these nations established a degree of prominence in world cinema.

CINEMA IN SPAIN AND MEXICO

Of the smaller film industries of the West, Spain's should be noted because it produced one of the world's greatest satirists in Luis Buñuel, and Mexico's should be commended because it allowed Buñuel to work after he was forced out of Spain by the fascists. (Buñuel also worked frequently in France.) In a career that spanned most of film history, Buñuel directed scores of brilliantly sardonic films that assaulted the institutions of bourgeois Christian culture and Western civilization. Among his most successful are *Los olvidados* (1950; *The Forgotten Ones*), *Él* (1952; *Torment*), *Nazarín* (1958), *Viridiana* (1961), *El ángel exterminador* (1962; *The Exterminating Angel*), *Belle de jour* (1967), *Le Charme discret de la bourgeoisie* (1973; *The Discreet Charm of the Bourgeoisie*), and *Le Fantôme de la liberté* (1974; *The Phantom of Liberty*). Buñuel deeply influenced Carlos Saura, another Spanish filmmaker whose work tended toward the grotesque and darkly comic (*La caza* [*The Hunt*], 1966; *La prima Angélica* [*Cousin Angelica*], 1974; *Bodas de sangre* [*Blood Wedding*], 1981), as well as an entire generation of younger directors who began to work after Spanish dictator Francisco Franco's death in 1975 (e.g., Victor Erice, Manuel Gutiérrez Aragón, Jaime Chavarri, and Pilar Miró). Pedro Almodóvar, whose provocative postmodernist works include *Mujeres al borde de un ataque de nervios* (1988; *Women on the Verge of a Nervous Breakdown*), *Todo sobre mi madre* (1999; *All About My Mother*), and *Habla con ella* (2002; *Talk to Her*), was hailed as Spain's most innovative director since Buñuel.

Buñuel's presence in Mexico between 1946 and 1965 had little effect on the general mediocrity of that nation's film industry, however. The commercialism of the Mexican cinema was briefly mitigated by a group of idealistic young filmmakers in the late 1960s (Arturo Ripstein, Felipe Cazals, Jaime Humberto Hermosillo) but reappeared even more relentlessly in the following decade. The Mexican cinema enjoyed a resurgence at the turn of the 21st century, and directors such as Alfonso Cuarón (*Y tu mamá también*, 2001) and Alejandro González Iñárritu (*Amores perros*, 2000) gained international acclaim.

CINEMA IN SWEDEN

The post-World War II Swedish cinema, like the Spanish, is noted for producing a single exceptional talent: Ingmar Bergman. Bergman first won international acclaim in the 1950s for his masterworks *Det sjunde inseglet* (1957; *The Seventh Seal*), *Smultronstället* (1957; *Wild Strawberries*), and *Jungfrukällan* (1960; *The Virgin Spring*). His trilogies of the 1960s—*Såsom i en spegel* (1961; *Through a Glass Darkly*), *Nattvardsgästerna* (1963; *Winter Light*), and *Tystnaden* (1963; *The Silence*); *Persona* (1966),

Vargtimmen (1968; *Hour of the Wolf*), and *Skammen* (1968; *Shame*)—were marked by a deep spiritual and intellectual probing, and later films, such as *Viskningar och rop* (1972; *Cries and Whispers*) and *Fanny och Alexander* (1984; *Fanny and Alexander*), confirmed that he is essentially a religious artist. Throughout the 20th century, the Scandinavian film industries remained small, state-subsidized, and (after the introduction of sound) oriented largely toward the domestic market.

CINEMA IN THE UNITED STATES

In the United States, as elsewhere, the last half of the 1960s was a time of intense conflict between generations and of rapid social change. Deeply involved with its own financial crisis, Hollywood was slow to respond to this new environment, and the studios made increasingly desperate attempts to attract a demographically homogeneous audience that no longer existed. The stupendous failure of Twentieth Century–Fox's blockbuster *Cleopatra* (1963) was briefly offset by the unexpected success of its *The Sound of Music* (1965), but over the next few years one box-office disaster after another threatened the studios' independence until most were absorbed by conglomerates. RKO had been sold to the General Tire and Rubber Corporation in 1955, and Universal had been acquired by MCA (the Music Corporation of America) in 1962. Paramount was then taken over by Gulf + Western Inc. in 1966, United Artists by Transamerica Corporation in 1967, Warner Bros. by Kinney National Services, Inc. (later renamed Warner Communications), in 1969, and MGM by the Las Vegas financier Kirk Kerkorian in 1970. Continuing this trend, in 1981 Twentieth Century–Fox was acquired by Denver oil tycoon Marvin Davis (who later shared ownership with publisher Rupert Murdoch), and Columbia was purchased by the Coca-Cola Company in 1982. United Artists merged with MGM in 1981 to form MGM/UA, which was subsequently acquired by Turner Broadcasting System, Inc., in 1986. The impact of such mergers was pronounced because they reduced filmmaking in the United States to a subordinate role; in the profit-making machinery of these multinational corporations, film production was often less important than the production of such items as refined sugar, ball bearings, field ammunition, rubber tires, and soft drinks.

Before conglomeration had completely restructured the industry, however, there was an exciting period of experimentation as Hollywood made various attempts to attract a new audience among the nation's youth. In an effort to lure members of the first "television generation" into movie theatres, the studios even recruited directors from the rival medium, such as Irvin Kershner (*A Fine Madness*, 1966), John Frankenheimer (*Seconds*, 1966), Sidney Lumet (*The Pawnbroker*, 1965), Robert Altman (*Countdown*, 1968), Arthur Penn (*Mickey One*, 1965), and Sam Peckinpah (*Major Dundee*, 1965). These directors collaborated with film-school-trained cinematographers (including Conrad Hall, Haskell Wexler, and William Fraker), as well as with the Hungarian-born cinematographers Laszlo Kovacs and Vilmos Zsigmond, to bring the heightened cinematic consciousness of the French New Wave to the American screen. Their films frequently exhibited unprecedented political and social consciousness as well.

THE YOUTH CULT AND OTHER TRENDS OF THE LATE 1960S

The years 1967–69 marked a turning point in American film history as Penn's *Bonnie and Clyde* (1967), Stanley Kubrick's *2001: A Space Odyssey* (1968), Peckinpah's *The Wild Bunch* (1969), Wexler's *Medium Cool* (1969), and Dennis Hopper's *Easy Rider* (1969) attracted the youth market to theatres in record numbers. (Altman's *M*A*S*H* [1970] provided

Peter Fonda (*left*) and Dennis Hopper in *Easy Rider* (1969), directed by Dennis Hopper.

a novel comedic coda to the quintet.) The films were unequal aesthetically (the first three being major revisions of their genres, the last two canny exploitations of the prevailing

mood), but all shared a cynicism toward established values and a fascination with apocalyptic violence. There was a sense, however briefly, that such films might provide the catalyst for a cultural revolution. Artistically, the films domesticated New Wave camera and editing techniques, enabling once-radical practices to enter the mainstream narrative cinema. Financially, they were so successful (*Easy Rider*, for example, returned $50,000,000 on a $375,000 investment) that producers quickly saturated the market with low-budget youth-culture movies, only a few of which—Penn's *Alice's Restaurant* (1969), Michael Wadleigh's *Woodstock* (1970), and David Maysles and Albert Maysles's *Gimme Shelter* (1970)—achieved even limited distinction.

Concurrent with the youth-cult boom was the new permissiveness toward sex made possible by the institution of the Motion Picture Association of America (MPAA) ratings system in 1968. Unlike the Production Code, this system of self-regulation did not prescribe the content of films but merely categorized them according to their appropriateness for young viewers. (G designates general audiences; PG suggests parental guidance; PG-13 strongly cautions parents because the film contains material inappropriate for children under 13; R indicates that the film is restricted to adults and to persons under 17 accompanied by a parent or guardian; and X or NC-17 signifies that no one under 17 may be admitted to the film—NC meaning "no children." In practice, the X rating has usually been given to unabashed pornography and the G rating to children's films, which has had the effect of concentrating sexually explicit but serious films in the R and NC-17 categories.) The introduction of the ratings system led immediately to the production of serious, nonexploitative adult films, such as John Schlesinger's *Midnight Cowboy* (1969) and Mike Nichols's *Carnal Knowledge* (1971), in which sexuality was treated with a maturity and realism unprecedented on the American screen.

The revolution that some had predicted would overturn American cinema, as well as American society, during the late 1960s never took place. Conglomeration and inflation did occur, however, especially between 1972 and 1979, when the average cost per feature increased by more than 500 percent to reach

$11 million in 1980. Despite the increasing costs, the unprecedented popularity of a few films (Francis Ford Coppola's *The Godfather*, 1972; Steven Spielberg's *Jaws*, 1975; George Lucas's *Star Wars*, 1977) produced enormous profits and stimulated a wildcat mentality within the industry. In this environment, it was not uncommon for the major companies to invest their working capital in the production of only five or six films a year, hoping that one or two would be extremely successful. At one point, Columbia reputedly had all of its assets invested in Spielberg's *Close Encounters of the Third Kind* (1977), a gamble that paid off handsomely; United Artists' similar investment in Michael Cimino's financially disastrous *Heaven's Gate* (1980), however, led to the sale of the company and its virtual destruction as a corporate entity.

The new generation of directors that came to prominence at this time included many who had been trained in university film schools—Francis Ford Coppola and Paul Schrader at the University of California, Los Angeles, George Lucas and John Milius at the University of Southern California, Martin Scorsese and Brian De Palma at New York University, Spielberg at California State College—as well as others who had been documentarians and critics before making their first features (Peter Bogdanovich, William Friedkin). These filmmakers brought to their work a technical sophistication and a sense of film history eminently suited to the new Hollywood, whose quest for enormously profitable films demanded slick professionalism and a thorough understanding of popular genres. The directors achieved success as highly skilled technicians in the production of cinematic thrills, although many were serious artists as well.

The graphic representation of violence and sex, which had been pioneered with risk by *Bonnie and Clyde*, *The Wild Bunch*, and *Midnight Cowboy* in the late 1960s, was exploited for its sensational effect during the '70s in such well-produced R-rated features as Coppola's *The Godfather*, Friedkin's *The Exorcist* (1973), Spielberg's *Jaws*, Scorsese's *Taxi Driver* (1976), De Palma's *Carrie* (1976), and scores of lesser films. The newly popular science-fiction/adventure genre was similarly supercharged through computer-enhanced special effects and Dolby sound as the brooding philosophical musings of Kubrick's *2001* gave way to the cartoon-strip violence of

Piper Laurie (holding knife) and Sissy Spacek in *Carrie* (1976), directed by Brian De Palma.

Lucas's *Star Wars*, Spielberg's *Raiders of the Lost Ark* (1981), and their myriad sequels and copies. There was, however, originality in the continuing work of veterans Altman (*McCabe and Mrs. Miller*, 1971; *Nashville*, 1975; *Three Women*, 1977) and Kubrick (*A Clockwork Orange*, 1971; *The Shining*, 1980), American Film Institute graduate Terrence Malick (*Badlands*, 1973; *Days of Heaven*, 1978), and controversial newcomer Cimino (*The Deerhunter*, 1978; *Heaven's Gate*). In addition, Coppola (*The Godfather*; *The Godfather, Part II*, 1974; *Apocalypse Now*, 1979) and Scorsese (*Mean Streets*, 1973; *Raging Bull*, 1980) created films of unassailable importance. Some of the strongest films of the era came from émigré directors working within the American industry—John Boorman's *Deliverance* (1972), Roman Polanski's *Chinatown* (1974), Miloš Forman's *One Flew over the Cuckoo's Nest* (1975), and Ridley Scott's *Alien* (1979). In general, however, Hollywood's new corporate managers lacked the judgment of industry veterans and tended to rely on the recently tried and true (producing an unprecedented number of high-budget sequels) and the viscerally sensational.

To this latter category belong the spate of "psycho-slasher" films that glutted the market in the wake of John Carpenter's highly successful low-budget chiller *Halloween* (1978). The formula for producing films of this type begins with the serial murder of teenagers by a ruthless psychotic and adds gratuitous sex and violence, with realistic gore provided by state-of-the-art makeup and special-effects artists. Its success was confirmed by the record-breaking receipts of the clumsily made *Friday the Thirteenth* (1980). There were precedents for psycho-killer violence in Hitchcock's *Psycho* (1960) and Tobe Hooper's *The Texas Chainsaw Massacre* (1974), but for decades the exploitation of gore had existed only at the periphery of the industry (in the "splatter" movies of Herschell Gordon Lewis, for example). The slasher films took the gore and violence into the mainstream of Hollywood films.

THE EFFECT OF NEW TECHNOLOGIES

During the 1980s the fortunes of the American film industry were increasingly shaped by new technologies of video delivery and imaging. Cable networks, direct-broadcast satellites, and half-inch videocassettes provided new means of motion-picture distribution, and computer-generated graphics provided new means of production, especially of special effects, forecasting the prospect of a fully automated "electronic cinema." Many studios, including Universal and Columbia, devoted the majority of their schedules to the production of telefilms for the commercial television networks, and nearly all the studios presold their theatrical features for cable and videocassette distribution. In fact, Tri-Star, one of Hollywood's major producer-distributors, was a joint venture of CBS Inc., Columbia Pictures, and Time-Life's premium cable service Home Box Office (HBO). HBO and competitor Showtime both functioned as producer-distributors in their own right by directly financing films and entertainment specials for cable television. In 1985, for the first time since the 1910s, independent film producers released more motion pictures than the major studios, largely to satisfy the demands of the cable and home-video markets.

The strength of the cable and video industries led producers to seek properties with video or "televisual" features that would play well on the small television screen (*Flashdance*, 1983; *Footloose*, 1984) or to attempt to draw audiences into the theatres with the promise of spectacular 70-mm photography and multitrack Dolby sound (*Amadeus*, 1984; *Aliens*, 1986). Ironically, the long-standing 35-mm theatrical feature survived in the mid-1980s in such unexpected places as "kidpix" (a form originally created to exploit the PG-13 rating when it was instituted in 1984—*The Breakfast Club*, 1985; *Stand by Me*, 1986) and, more dramatically, the Vietnam combat film (Oliver Stone's *Platoon*, 1986; Coppola's *Gardens of*

Stone, 1987; Kubrick's *Full Metal Jacket*, 1987). Responding to the political climate, the studios produced some of their most jingoistic films since the Korean War, endorsing the notion of political betrayal in Vietnam (*Rambo: First Blood, Part II*, 1985), fear of a Soviet invasion (*Red Dawn*, 1985), and military vigilantism (*Top Gun*, 1986). Films with a "literary" quality, many of them British-made, were also popular in the American market during the 1980s (*A Passage to India*, 1984; *A Room with a View*, 1985; *Out of Africa*, 1985).

These trends were taken to greater extremes in the 1990s and beyond, to the extent that the style and content of a film determined its most popular venue. Major advances in computer-generated animation and special effects allowed for films of unprecedented visual sophistication (*Jurassic Park*, 1993; *Star Wars: Episode I—The Phantom Menace*, 1999; *The Matrix*, 1999), and audiences preferred the experience of seeing such films on large theatre screens. Computer animation was also put to good use in films that play equally well on theatre or television screens, such as *Toy Story* (1995), *Antz* (1998), and *Chicken Run* (2000). Independent producers, especially those who specialized in low-budget films of intimate subject matter, regained strength under the new regime of home video and created some of the most unconventional and interesting work the American cinema had seen in some time; they included the Coen brothers, Joel and Ethan (*Blood Simple*, 1984; *Fargo*, 1996; *O Brother, Where Art Thou?*, 2000), Spike Jonze (*Being John Malkovich*, 1999; *Adaptation*, 2002), and Quentin Tarantino (*Pulp Fiction*, 1994; *Jackie Brown*, 1997). It was also an era in which low-cost marketing via the Internet could turn a $50,000 independent film into a $100,000,000 blockbuster (*The Blair Witch Project*, 1999). These "indie" films were too original to have been made in the studio era and too eccentric for the mass-market economies of the late 20th century. They harkened back to the vitality and integrity of the pre-studio age—to the work of D.W. Griffith, Buster Keaton, Erich von Stroheim, and Charlie Chaplin—when anything was possible because everything was new.

CHAPTER FIVE

TRANSITION TO THE 21ST CENTURY: THE EXPANSION OF MEDIA CULTURE

The history of motion pictures in the last period of the 20th century and the beginning of the 21st was shaped in part by new technologies and the expansion of media culture that such technologies fostered. In the 1980s, for example, the widespread adoption of the videocassette recorder (VCR) opened up new possibilities for the distribution of films as videocassettes, giving wider circulation and easier access to works made throughout the world. In the same manner, new cable and satellite television systems that delivered media directly to homes created additional markets for film distribution and income sources for film producers. With the availability of higher-quality video cameras, more filmmakers used video technology to lower production costs, later transferring the image to film stock for theatrical exhibition. In the following years, the spread and increasing capabilities of computer animation as well as digital video cameras and DVDs (digital video discs) accelerated these trends, with the computer emerging as a new production unit in filmmaking and the Internet as a site for film distribution and exhibition. One result of these changes was the appearance on the world stage of filmmakers—particularly Chinese-language ones—from places that had previously been little recognized within international film culture.

CHINESE CINEMA

Filmmaking had become nearly moribund in China from the mid-1960s to the mid-1970s during the Cultural Revolution. Under new leadership in the late 1970s, the ruling Chinese Communist Party sought to instigate economic development and open the country to international commerce and communication. Some veteran filmmakers resumed their careers, and one, Xie Jin, made a controversial work, *Furong zhen* (1986; *Hibiscus Town*), showing the deleterious effects of communist political dogma on a rural village. The Beijing Film Academy, closed for more than a decade, reopened in 1978 and graduated its first new class in 1982. From this group came several figures who began to make films in the

1980s and who became known collectively as China's Fifth Generation of film directors (the previous four generations had been associated with specific decades beginning in the 1910s and early '20s).

The Fifth Generation significantly transformed Chinese cinema by moving production away from its traditional studio interiors and backlot standing sets and into distant rural locations, which the filmmakers in many cases had come to know when they were sent from the cities during the Cultural Revolution to be country teachers or farmhands. Chen Kaige's *Huang tudi* (1984; *Yellow Earth*), *Da yuebing* (1986; *The Big Parade*), *Haizi wang* (1987; *King of the Children*), and *Bian zou bian chang* (1991; *Life on a String*) emphasized China's wide-open spaces and bright landscape colours. Similar impulses, with variations of style and theme, shaped the work of Zhang Yimou (*Hong gaoliang* [1987; *Red Sorghum*], *Ju Dou* [1990], *Dahong denglong gaogao gua* [1991; *Raise the Red Lantern*], *Qiu Ju da guansi* [1992; *The Story of Qiu Ju*]) and Tian Zhuangzhuang (*Lie chang zha sha* [1985; *On the Hunting Ground*], *Daoma zei* [1986; *Horse Thief*]).

As these filmmakers, and others, gained international recognition, their work became both more commercial and more political and thus more controversial in the eyes of Chinese authorities. The Cultural Revolution became a

A scene from *Farewell My Concubine* (1993), directed by Chen Kaige.

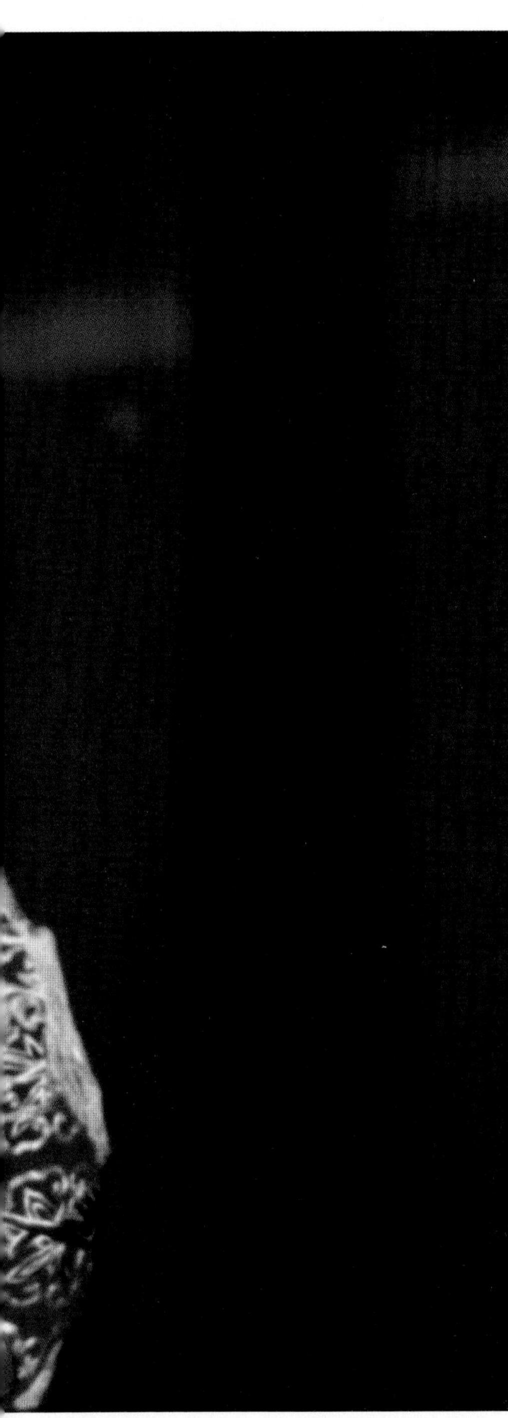

subject in Chen's *Bawang bieji* (1993; *Farewell My Concubine*), Zhang's *Huozhe* (1994; *To Live*), and Tian's *Lan fenzheng* (1993; *The Blue Kite*), the last of which caused the filmmaker to be banned temporarily from film work. Both Chen and Zhang turned to what may have appeared a less-contentious historical subject, Shanghai in the early 20th century, although possibly with allegorical purpose, in the former's *Fengyue* (1996; *Temptress Moon*, 1996) and the latter's *Yao a yao yao dao waipo qiao* (1995; *Shanghai Triad*). As these filmmakers continued to develop in new directions (and Tian was able to resume film work), younger directors identified as a Sixth Generation, often working independently of the official studios, focused on contemporary urban subjects, depicting the social issues involved in the rapid growth of China's cities.

THE IRANIAN REVOLUTION: CINEMA IN IRAN

The most surprising rise to prominence of a little-known national cinema during the late 20th century, at least from an outside perspective, occurred in the case of Iran. In the aftermath of the Iranian Revolution (1978–79), some 200 film theatres were destroyed in a campaign against secular media and Western cultural influence, but religious authorities eventually decreed that motion pictures could be valuable for educational purposes. With Hollywood films banned, Iranian filmmakers developed a quiet, contemplative style that mixed actuality and fiction and often involved children as performers and centres of the narrative. Abbas Kiarostami, who before the revolution had made short films for the Institute for the Intellectual Development of Children and Young Adults in Iran, gained international acclaim as an avatar of this distinctly Iranian style with films such as *Khaneh-ye doost kojast?* (1987; *Where Is My Friend's House?*), *Zendegi va digar hich* (1992; *And Life Goes On*), *Zir-e darakhtan-e zitun* (1994; *Through the Olive Trees*), *Ta'm e guilass* (1997; *Taste of Cherry*), and *Bad mara khahad bourd* (1999; *The Wind Will Carry Us*). For *Nema-ye Nazdik* (1989; *Close-Up*), people who were involved in an actual public incident restaged the events for Kiarostami's camera, a further innovation that filmmakers in Iran and elsewhere emulated.

Moshen Makhmalbaf made his name as a director of such films as *Salaam Cinema* (1995), *Nun va goldoon* (1996; *A Moment of Innocence*), and the visually stunning *Gabbeh* (1996), and he also served as screenwriter and producer for other family members. Samira Makhmalbaf, his daughter, made a striking debut as a director at age 17 with *Sib* (1998; *The Apple*), and Marzieh Meshkini, his wife, made the film *Roozi keh zan shodam* (2000; *The Day I Became a Woman*), her first. Other Iranian filmmakers whose works have had international success include Jafar Panahi, with *Badkonak-e sefid* (1995; *The White Balloon*), *Dayereh* (2000; *The Circle*), and *Offside* (2006), and Majid Majidi, director of *Bachela-Ya aseman* (1997; *Children of Heaven*) and Rang-e khoda (1999; *The Color of Heaven*).

EUROPEAN CINEMA

At the end of the 20th century, the notion of national cinemas had become problematic in many of the traditional film cultures of western Europe. This is not to say that national cinemas had ceased to exist—the situation of France would contradict such an assertion—but that the trends toward international coproduction and toward filmmakers and performers working in different countries and languages had reached a stage where coherent film movements identified with a particular national culture, such as Italian Neorealism, the French New Wave, or New German Cinema, had become difficult to identify or sustain. A film such as *Heaven* (2002), cowritten by the Polish filmmaker Krzysztof Kieslowski, with Tom Tykwer from Germany as director, set in Italy and spoken in Italian and English by American and Australian lead actors, seemed the rule rather than the exception. Even as many countries produced substantial numbers of films, the idea of nationality was exemplified more by singular individuals than by wider groupings.

Among the outstanding figures of European cinema were Pedro Almodóvar of Spain, Manoel de Oliveira of Portugal, Théo Angelopoulos of Greece, Aki Kaurismäki of Finland, and Nanni Moretti of Italy. Almodóvar, who had broken sexual taboos in his early work, entered a mature period of great human subtlety and complexity in the 1990s and 2000s with such works as *La flor de mi secreto* (1995; *The Flower of My Secret*), *Carne trémula* (1997; *Live Flesh*), *Todo sobre mi madre* (1999; *All About My Mother*), and *Habla con ella* (2002; *Talk to Her*). Oliveira—who was born in 1908, made his first films in the 1930s, and was artistically restricted for years by the Portuguese dictatorship—was still directing at age 100. He had perhaps his most productive period after 1990, with such films as *Vale Abraão* (1993; *Abraham's Valley*) and *Viagem ao princípio do mundo* (1997; *Voyage to the Beginning of the World*), the latter starring Italian actor Marcello Mastroianni in his last screen role. Angelopoulos, a master of Greek cinema since his first feature film in 1970, made several ambitious works fusing the personal and the historical: *To Vlemma tou Odyssea* (1995; *Ulysses' Gaze*) and Mia aeoniotita ke mia mera (1998; *Eternity and a Day*). Kaurismäki, one of Europe's most cosmopolitan filmmakers, returned to Finnish themes in *Kauas pilvet karkaavat* (1996; *Drifting Clouds*) and *Mies vailla menneisyyttä* (2002; *The Man Without a Past*). Moretti became a popular figure in Italy by writing, directing, and performing in his own films, of which *Caro diario* (1993; *Dear Diary*) was exemplary.

The one concerted effort to launch a film movement in Europe came from a filmmakers' collective in Denmark, which unveiled a doctrine called Dogme 95 (Dogma

95) at the Cannes film festival in 1998. The 10 rules of the Dogme manifesto argued against technological gadgetry in cinema and for a straightforward realism in style and content. A leader of the group was Lars von Trier, a Danish director whose films include the English-language *Breaking the Waves* (1996). The first Dogme work, *Festen* (1998; *The Celebration*), directed by Thomas Vinterberg, was well received, and dozens of films were subsequently released under the movement's banner, including works by American and French directors as well as by Danes.

EASTERN EUROPE AND RUSSIA

With the fall of the Berlin Wall in 1989 and the collapse of the Soviet Union two years later, the film cultures of Russia and the former Soviet-bloc countries of eastern Europe experienced dramatic transformations. Formerly controlled and supported by the state, film production shifted into private hands. With the boundaries that previously had divided eastern from western Europe now torn down, filmmakers were freed to work where they pleased or where opportunities existed. A prominent example was the Polish director Krzysztof Kieslowski, who in 1991 made

La Double Vie de Véronique (*The Double Life of Veronique*), which suggested a mysterious symmetry between two women, one living in Poland and the other in France. Kieslowski shifted his filmmaking work to France, where he made the important *Trois couleurs* ("Three Colours") trilogy—*Bleu* (1993; *Blue*), *Rouge* (1994; *Red*), and *Blanc* (1994; *White*)—before his death in 1996.

Scene from *The Double Life of Veronique* (1991), directed by Krzysztof Kieslowski.

In Russia a significant figure to emerge was Aleksandr Sokurov, whose early films had been "shelved," or prohibited from public screening, until 1987. Sokurov's first film to be widely seen internationally was *Mat' i syn* (1997; *Mother and Son*). In 2002 he made *Russki kovcheg* (*Russian Ark*), a 96-minute tour of the Hermitage museum in St. Petersburg, in a single take without cuts, the longest Steadicam shot ever recorded. Aleksey Balabanov directed both crime dramas—*Brat* (1997; *Brother*) and a sequel, *Brat II* (2000; Brother II)—and meditative historical works, including *Pro ourodov I lioudiei* (1998; *Of Freaks and Men*).

Filmmaking was inevitably affected by the prolonged, bitter, and brutal breakup of Yugoslavia during the 1990s. Under the circumstances, every film from the region was likely to come under attack from some group as a work of propaganda. This was the case for the work of Emir Kusturica, who had gained wide recognition for his films in the 1980s but caused controversy in the 1990s with *Underground* (1995) and *Crna macka, beli macor* (1998; *Black Cat, White Cat*).

AUSTRALIA, NEW ZEALAND, AND CANADA

In the late 20th century it sometimes seemed that Australian and New Zealand filmmakers were more active in Hollywood than in their home countries. Many Hollywood blockbusters, with leading actors such as Mel Gibson and prominent directors such as Phillip Noyce, had a strong Australian influence. The most prominent figure to remain outside the Hollywood orbit was Jane Campion, born in New Zealand and based in Australia, whose films include *Sweetie* (1989), *An Angel at My Table* (1990), *The Piano* (1993), *The Portrait of a Lady* (1996), and *Holy Smoke* (1999). In New Zealand Peter Jackson made his mark with the horror comedies *Bad Taste* (1987), *Meet the Feebles* (1990), *Braindead* (1992; released in the United States as *Dead Alive*), and *The Frighteners* (1996), along with an impressive art film about a 1950s murder case, *Heavenly Creatures* (1994). He directed one of the most extensive projects in Hollywood's history, an adaptation of the classic fantasy novel *The Lord of the Rings* by English author J.R.R. Tolkien. All three parts of Tolkien's trilogy were shot at the same time in New Zealand and later released as *The Fellowship of the Ring* (2001), *The*

Peter Jackson directs Naomi Watts in a scene from *King Kong* (2005).

Two Towers (2002), and *The Return of the King* (2003). He also cowrote and directed a remake of *King Kong* (2005).

The situation was the same for English-language filmmakers in Canada, although Hollywood's lure affected Canadian performers more than directors. Canadian filmmakers of note included Atom Egoyan, whose work in the 1990s included *The Adjuster* (1991), *Exotica* (1994), *The Sweet Hereafter* (1997), and *Felicia's Journey* (1999), and David Cronenberg, who in the same period made *Naked Lunch* (1991), *M. Butterfly* (1993), *Crash* (1996), and *eXistenZ* (1999). Filmmaking in Quebec, which had gone through a strong period in the 1970s and '80s, made a lesser impression in the 1990s. Denys Arcand, a key figure of the earlier period with such works as *Le Déclin de l'empire américain* (1986; *The Decline of the American Empire*) and *Jésus de Montréal* (1989; *Jesus of Montreal*), made *Love and Human Remains* (1993) and *Stardom* (2000) in English. His *Les Invasions barbares* (2003; *The Barbarian Invasions*) won an Academy Award for best foreign-language film.

MEXICO

Mexican cinema was representative of many national film cultures that had, as it were, one foot in its own language and film traditions and the other connected to influences from and opportunities in Hollywood. The actor Alfonso Arau directed a highly popular film based on a novel written by his wife, Laura Esquivel, *Como agua para chocolate* (1992; *Like Water for Chocolate*). He then went on to be a director in American film and television. Alfonso Cuarón, who had been working in Hollywood, returned to Mexico to direct the acclaimed *Y tu mamá también* (2001). Among those who remained in Mexico were Arturo Ripstein, director, among other works, of *Profundo carmesi* (1996; *Deep Crimson*) and *El coronel no tiene quien le escriba* (1999; *No One Writes to the Colonel*), and Alejandro González Iñárritu, who made *Amores perros* (2000) and *Babel* (2006). The success of nearly all these works as international art films was a sign that, despite Hollywood's dominance of the world film marketplace, there was still a place for distinctive national visions in cinema at the turn of the 21st century.

UNITED STATES

In the last years of the 20th century and the early years of the 21st, the idea of "synergy" dominated the motion-picture industry in the United States, and an unprecedented wave of mergers and acquisitions pursued this ultimately elusive concept. Simply put, synergy implied that consolidating related media and entertainment properties under a single umbrella could strengthen every facet of a coordinated communications empire. Motion pictures, broadcast television, cable and satellite systems, radio networks, theme parks, newspapers and magazines, book publishers, manufacturers of home entertainment products, sports teams, Internet service providers—these were among the different elements that came together in various corporate combinations under the notion that each would boost the others. News Corporation Ltd., originally an Australian media company, started the trend by acquiring Twentieth Century–Fox in 1985. The Japanese manufacturing giant Sony Corporation acquired Columbia Pictures Entertainment, Inc., from The Coca-Cola Company in 1989. Another Japanese firm, Matsushita, purchased Universal Studios (as part of Music Corporation of America, or MCA) in 1990; it then was acquired by Seagram Company Ltd. (1995), became part of Vivendi Universal Entertainment (2000), and merged with the National Broadcasting Co., Inc. (2004), a subsidiary of General Electric Company. Paramount Pictures, as Paramount Communications, Inc., became part of Viacom Inc. In perhaps the most striking of all ventures, Warner Communications merged with Time

Inc. to become Time Warner Inc., which in turn came together with the Internet company America Online (AOL) to form AOL Time Warner in 2001. The company then changed its name again, back to Time Warner Inc., in 2003, a year after the company suffered a quarterly loss that was at that time the largest ever reported by an American company. The Disney Company itself became an acquirer, adding Miramax Films, the television network American Broadcasting Company, and the cable sports network ESPN, among other properties. The volume of corporate reshuffling and realignment had an undoubted impact on the studios involved. Nevertheless, the potential for success of such synergistic entities—and, more particularly, the positive or negative effect on their motion-picture units—remained an open question.

It could well be argued, however, that motion-picture companies' corporate links with the wider media world and emergent communications forms such as the Internet fostered receptivity to new technologies that rapidly transformed film production in the 1990s and into the 21st century. As early as 1982, the Disney film *Tron* made extensive use of computer-generated images, which were introduced in a short special-effects sequence in which a human character is deconstructed into electronic particles and reassembled inside a computer. A few years later computer-generated imagery was greatly facilitated when it became possible to transfer film images into a computer and manipulate them digitally. The possibilities became apparent in director James Cameron's *Terminator 2: Judgment Day* (1991), in images of the shape-changing character T-1000.

In the 1990s, computer-generated imagery made rapid strides and became a standard feature not only of Hollywood action-adventure films but also of nearly any work that required special visual effects. Examples of landmark films utilizing the new technologies included Steven Spielberg's *Jurassic Park* (1993); *Independence Day* (1996), directed by Roland Emmerich; and *The Matrix* (1999), written and directed by Larry (later Lana) Wachowski and Andy Wachowski. In Spielberg's film, based on a best-selling novel by Michael Crichton, a number of long-extinct dinosaur species are re-created through genetic engineering. At the special-effects firm Industrial Light and Magic, models of the dinosaurs were scanned into computers and animated realistically to produce the first computer-generated images of lifelike action, rather than fantasy scenes. In *Independence Day*, a film combining the science-fiction and disaster genres in which giant alien spaceships attack Earth, an air battle was programmed in a computer so that each individual aircraft maneuvered, fired its weapons, and dueled with other flying objects in intricate patterns of action that would have been too time-consuming and costly to achieve by traditional special-effects means. By the end of the 1990s, the developing new technologies were displayed perhaps more fully than ever before in the Wachowskis' spectacular film, in which the computer functions as both a central subject and a primary visual tool. For a scene in which actor Keanu Reeves appears to be dodging bullets that pass by him in a visible slow-motion trajectory, a computer program determined what motion-picture and still images were to be photographed, and then the computer assembled the images into a complete visual sequence.

In part through the expensive and lavish effects attained through the new technologies, American cinema at the end of the 20th century sustained and even widened its domination of the world film marketplace. Domestically, the expansion of ancillary products and venues—which during the 1990s were dominated by the sale and rental of video cassettes and then DVDs for home viewing as well as by additional cable and satellite outlets for movie presentation—produced new revenues that were becoming equal to, or in some cases more important than, income from theatrical exhibition. Nevertheless, exhibition outlets continued to grow, with new "megaplex" theatres offering several dozen cinemas, while distribution strategies called for opening major commercial films on 1,000 or more—sometimes as many as 3,000 by the late 1990s—screens across the country. The competition for box-office returns became something of a spectator sport, with the media reporting every Monday on the previous weekend's multimillion-dollar grosses and ranking the top-10 films by ticket sales. The exhibition environment seemed to demand more than ever that film production be geared to the tastes of teenage spectators who frequented the suburban mall cinemas on weekends, and commentators within the industry as well as outside it observed what they regarded as the diminished quality of mainstream films. As if reflecting that judgment, in 1996 only one major studio film, *Jerry Maguire*, was among the five nominees for best picture at the annual Academy of Motion Picture Arts and Sciences awards ceremony (the other nominees were an American independent film, *Fargo*; an Australian work, *Shine*; a film from Britain, *Secrets & Lies*; and the winner, an international production with British stars and based on a novel written by a Canadian, *The English Patient*).

The motion-picture industry's emphasis on pleasing the youth audience with special effects-laden blockbusters and genre works such as teen-oriented horror films and comedies inevitably diminished the role of directors as dominant figures in the creative process, further reducing the status that Hollywood directors had attained in the auteur-oriented 1960s and '70s. Still, more than a handful of filmmakers, several of them veterans of that earlier era, maintained their prestige as artists practicing in a commercial medium. Two of the most prominent, who had launched their careers in the early 1970s, were Steven Spielberg and Martin Scorsese. In addition to *Jurassic Park*, Spielberg's works in the 1990s include *Schindler's List* (1993, winner of an Academy Award for best picture), *Amistad*

Leonardo DiCaprio (*left*) and Jack Nicholson in *The Departed* (2006), directed by Martin Scorsese.

(1997), and *Saving Private Ryan* (1998), with *A.I. Artificial Intelligence* (2001) and *Munich* (2005) among his subsequent films. Scorsese directed *GoodFellas* (1990), *The Age of Innocence* (1993), *Casino* (1995), *Kundun* (1997), *Gangs of New York* (2002), and *The Departed* (2006; winner of an Academy Award for best picture).

The actor-director Clint Eastwood was also prolific in this period, winning the best picture Academy Award with *Unforgiven* (1992) and directing such other films as *Midnight in the Garden of Good and Evil* (1997), *Mystic River* (2003), *Million Dollar Baby* (2004; Academy Award for best picture and best director), *Letters from Iwo Jima* (2006), and *Gran Torino* (2008). Stanley Kubrick died before the release of *Eyes Wide Shut* (1999), his first film since *Full Metal Jacket* (1987). Two decades passed between Terrence Malick's *Days of Heaven* (1978) and *The Thin Red Line* (1998).

A succeeding generation of filmmakers who could claim the status of auteur included such figures as David Lynch, Oliver Stone, James Cameron, and Spike Lee. Lynch's work in the 1990s and beyond includes *Lost Highway* (1996), *The Straight Story* (1999), *Mulholland Drive* (2001), and *Inland Empire* (2006). Stone, best known for politically oriented films such as *JFK* (1991), *Nixon* (1995), and *W.* (2008), also made *Natural Born Killers* (1994), *U-Turn* (1997),

Denzel Washington in *Malcolm X* (1992), directed by Spike Lee

and *Any Given Sunday* (1999). Cameron's *Titanic* (1997), re-creating the 1912 sinking of an ocean liner on its maiden voyage after striking an iceberg, won the Academy Award for best picture and broke domestic and worldwide box-office records. Lee, the most prominent among a group of young African American filmmakers who began working in mainstream cinema, was best known for *Do the Right Thing* (1989) and *Malcolm X* (1992); his many other films include *Crooklyn* (1994) and *Summer of Sam* (1999), along with documentaries such as *4 Little Girls* (1997), concerning the deaths of four young black girls in the bombing of a Birmingham, Alabama, church in 1963, and *When the Levees Broke* (2006), about New Orleans during and after Hurricane Katrina. Among newcomers who emerged during the 1990s, Paul Thomas Anderson stood out with *Boogie Nights* (1997), *Magnolia* (1999), *Punch-Drunk Love* (2002), and *There Will Be Blood* (2008).

Another significant development in late 20th-century American cinema was the emergence of a self-designated independent film movement. Its origins perhaps lay in the perceived diminution of opportunities for personal filmmaking in the post-1970s commercial industry. To take up the slack, organizations such as the Independent Feature Project and the Sundance Film Festival in Park City, Utah, were founded to encourage and promote independent work. A major breakthrough was achieved when an American independent film, *sex, lies and videotape* (1989), the first feature by Steven Soderbergh, won the top prize at the Cannes festival in France. (Soderbergh went on, like Spike Lee and others, to work on both independent and mainstream projects; he won an Academy Award as best director for *Traffic* [2000].) In the 1990s independent directors began to develop projects that were closer in style to popular Hollywood genres such as the gangster film and post-World War II film noir. These proved exceedingly popular with Cannes festival juries, who awarded their top prize to David Lynch's *Wild at Heart* in 1990, *Barton Fink* by the Coen brothers in 1991, and Quentin Tarantino's *Pulp Fiction* in 1994. Tarantino's other films include *Reservoir Dogs* (1992), *Jackie Brown* (1997), *Kill Bill: Vol. 1* (2003), and *Kill Bill: Vol. 2* (2004). Among the Coen brothers' works were *Miller's Crossing* (1990), *Fargo* (1995), *The Big Lebowski* (1998), *O Brother, Where Art Thou?* (2000), *The Man Who Wasn't There* (2001), and *No Country for Old Men* (2007; Academy Award for best picture).

Beyond this genre orientation, which cemented the popularity of independent films for many in the mainstream audience, the independent movement fostered what came to be called niche filmmaking, which generated works growing out of ethnic and identity movements in contemporary American culture. Among these were films by African American, Native American, and Chicano and Chicana filmmakers, as well as works representing feminist and gay and lesbian cultural viewpoints and experience. Documentary filmmaking from these and other perspectives also thrived in the independent world. Independent nonfiction films of significance included Errol Morris's *The Thin Blue Line* (1988), an exploration of a miscarriage of justice in a Dallas murder case; *Hoop Dreams* (1994), by Steve James, Frederick Marx, and Peter Gilbert, concerning the struggles of two young African American basketball hopefuls in Chicago; *Crumb* (1994), Terry Zwigoff's portrait of the underground comic book artist Robert Crumb; and *Buena Vista Social Club* (1999), Wim Wenders and Ry Cooder's rediscovery of old-time popular Cuban musicians.

The motion picture is a remarkably effective medium for conveying drama and, especially, evoking emotion. The art of motion pictures is exceedingly complex, requiring contributions from nearly all the other arts as well as countless technical skills (for example, in sound recording, photography, and optics). Emerging at the end of the 19th century, this new art form became one of the most popular and influential media of the 20th century and beyond.

As a commercial venture, offering fictional narratives to large audiences in theatres, the motion picture was quickly recognized as perhaps the first truly mass form of entertainment. Without losing its broad appeal, the medium also developed as a means of artistic expression in such areas as acting, directing, screenwriting, cinematography, costume and set design, and music.

The motion picture gives what has been called a strong sense of being present; the film image always appears to be in the present tense. There is also the concrete nature of film; it appears to show actual people and things.

No less important are the conditions under which the motion picture ideally is seen, where everything helps to dominate the spectators. They are taken from their everyday environment, partially isolated from others, and comfortably seated in a dark auditorium. The darkness concentrates their attention and prevents comparison of the image on the screen with surrounding objects or people. For a while, spectators live in the world the motion picture unfolds before them.

In its short history, the art of motion pictures has frequently undergone changes that seemed fundamental, such as those resulting from the introduction of sound. It exists today in styles that differ significantly from country to country and in forms as diverse as the documentary created by one person with a handheld camera and the multimillion-dollar epic involving hundreds of performers and technicians.

GLOSSARY

aesthetic Appreciative of, responsive to, or zealous about the beautiful; responsive to or appreciative of what is pleasurable to the senses.

anamorphic Producing, relating to, or marked by intentional distortion (as by unequal magnification along perpendicular axes) of an image.

atheism A disbelief in the existence of a deity.

austere Simple or plain; not fancy.

Bolshevik A member of the extremist wing of the Russian Social Democratic party that seized power in Russia by the Revolution of November 1917.

celluloid A motion-picture film.

classicism The principles or style embodied in the literature, art, or architecture of ancient Greece and Rome.

commercialism The attitude or actions of people who are influenced too strongly by the desire to earn money or buy goods rather than by other values.

Communism A doctrine based on revolutionary Marxian socialism and Marxism-Leninism that was the official ideology of the Union of Soviet Socialist Republics.

dialectic A method of examining and discussing opposing ideas in order to find the truth.

elitism The selectivity of the elite; snobbery.

Expressionism A theory or practice in art of seeking to depict the subjective emotions and responses that objects and events arouse in the artist.

fascism A way of organizing a society in which a government ruled by a dictator controls the lives of the people and in which people are not allowed to disagree with the government.

feudalism A social system that existed in Europe during the Middle Ages in which people worked and fought for nobles who gave them protection and the use of land in return.

formalism A method, style, way of thinking, etc., that shows very careful attention to traditional forms and rules.

Futurism A movement in art, music, and literature begun in Italy about 1909 and marked especially by an effort to give formal expression to the dynamic energy and movement of mechanical processes.

imagism A 20th-century movement in art advocating free verse and the expression of ideas and emotions through clear precise images.

jingoism The feelings and beliefs of people who think that their country is always right and who are in favor of aggressive acts against other countries.

lyricism A quality that expresses deep feelings or emotions in a work of art.

monopoly Complete control of the entire supply of goods or of a service in a certain area or market.

naturalistic Showing people or things as they really are.

propaganda Ideas or statements that are often false or exaggerated and that are spread in order to help a cause, a political leader, a government, etc.

Realism A style of art or literature that shows or describes people and things as they are in real life.

stereoscopic Used to describe an image that appears to have depth and solidness and that is created by using a special device (called a stereo-scope) to look at two slightly different photographs of something at the same time.

synchronous Recurring or operating at exactly the same periods.

vigilante A person who is not a police officer but who tries to catch and punish criminals.

xenophobia Fear or hatred of strangers or foreigners.

BIBLIOGRAPHY

GENERAL HISTORIES

The history of motion pictures is discussed generally in *Arthur Knight, The Liveliest Art: A Panoramic History of the Movies*, rev. ed. (1979), an influential history; Louis Giannetti and Scott Eyman, *Flashback: A Brief History of Film, 6th ed.* (2009), a concise overview with an emphasis on American film; Robert Sklar, *A World History of Film* (2002), a comprehensive survey that examines principal films, directors, and national cinemas; Paul Rotha, with Richard Griffith, *The Film till Now*, new ed. (1967), a substantial history, though now dimmed by age and a lack of critical perspective; Pierre Leprohon, *Histoire du cinéma*, 2 vol. (1961–63), a useful reference work of names, dates, titles, and events; Gerald Mast, *A Short History of the Movies*, 11th ed. (2011); David A. Cook, *A History of Narrative Film*, 4th ed. (2003), a wide-ranging historical survey of international film; Eric Rhode, *A History of the Cinema from Its Origins to 1970* (1976, reprinted 1985), an international critical history providing detailed though opinionated coverage; Kenneth Macgowan, *Behind the Screen: The History and Techniques of the Motion Picture* (1965), a dated but still valuable history by an industry insider; and Ephraim Katz, *The Film Encyclopedia*, 7th ed. (2012), an informative reference source. Perhaps the most exhaustive study of American film history is Charles Harpole (ed.), *History of the American Cinema* (1990–).

HISTORICAL STUDIES OF SPECIFIC PERIODS

Early developments are studied in Terry Ramsaye, *A Million and One Nights: A History of the Motion Picture*, 2 vol. (1926, reissued in 1 vol., 1986), a romantic account covering the period to 1925, with emphasis on American film between 1890 and 1915; *Michael Chanan, The Dream That Kicks: The Prehistory and Early Years of Cinema in Britain* (1980), an extraordinary study of the cultural and ideological "site" of cinema at the moment of its birth; Kevin Brownlow, *Hollywood, the Pioneers* (1979), a systematic treatment of the subject through the 1920s, copiously illustrated by John Kobal; John Fell (ed.), *Film Before Griffith* (1983); and Lary May, *Screening Out the Past: The Birth of Mass Culture and the Motion Picture Industry* (1980, reprinted 1983).

Further developments are presented in Georges Sadoul, *Histoire générale du cinéma*, 6 vol. in varied editions (1973–75), a detailed study of the epoch of silent film; Kevin Brownlow, T*he Parade's Gone By* (1968), a well-illustrated study of American silent films and stars, based on interviews with survivors; John Kobal, *Hollywood: The Years of Innocence* (1985), a pictorial work on the period; William K. Everson, *American Silent Film* (1978, reissued 1998); Graham Petrie, *Hollywood Destinies: European Directors in America, 1922–1931* (1985); and Benjamin B. Hampton, *A History of the Movies* (1931, reissued as *History of the American Film Industry from Its Beginnings to 1931*, 1970). An excellent, well-researched account of the coming of sound is found in Alexander Walker, *The Shattered Silents: How the Talkies Came to Stay* (1978, reissued 1986). See also Evan William Cameron (ed.), *Sound and the Cinema: The Coming of Sound to American Film* (1980), an anthology of scholarly essays and reminiscences; Leonard Quart and Albert Auster, *American Films and Society Since 1945* (1984), a brief, penetrating study; and William Luhr (ed.), *World Cinema Since 1945* (1987).

HISTORICAL AND CRITICAL STUDIES OF NATIONAL FILM MOVEMENTS

British filmmaking is the subject of Roy Armes, *A Critical History of the British Cinema* (1978); Rachael Low, *The History of the British Film*, 7 vol. (1948–79), a detailed study of the silent film; Ernest Betts, *The Film Business: A History of British Cinema, 1896–1972* (1973), a standard, compact history; Alexander Walker, *Hollywood UK: The British Film Industry in the Sixties* (1974; also published as *Hollywood, England*, 1974, reprinted 1986); George Perry, *The Great British Picture Show*, rev. ed. (1985), a popular concise history; and Sarah Street, *British National Cinema* (1997).

For France, see Richard Abel, *French Cinema: The First Wave, 1915–1929* (1984), a definitive scholarly study of avant-garde and commercial cinema of the era, superbly illustrated; James Monaco, *The New Wave: Truffaut, Godard, Chabrol, Rohmer, Rivette* (1976, reprinted 1980), an excellent critical study; Georges Sadoul, *French Film* (1953, reissued 1972); Roy Armes, *French Cinema* (1985); and Alan Williams, *Republic of Images: A History of French Filmmaking* (1992).

For Germany, see Siegfried Kracauer, *From Caligari to Hitler: A Psychological History of the German Film* (1947, reissued with additions, 1974), a psychological, sociological, and political analysis; David Stewart Hull, *Film in the Third Reich: A Study of the German Cinema, 1933–1945* (1969, reissued 1973), an exploration of the cinema's role in Nazi propaganda; David Welch, *Propaganda and the German Cinema*, 1933–1945 (1983); Julian Petley, *Capital and Culture: German Cinema, 1933–45* (1979), a discussion of the economic and social structure of the Nazi film industry; Lotte H. Eisner, *The Haunted Screen: Expressionism in the German Cinema and the Influence of Max Reinhardt* (1969, reissued 1973; originally published in French, 1965; new enlarged French ed., 1981), a study of the influence of the arts of painting, drama, and the novel on the cinema; and Eric Rentschler, *West German Film in the Course of Time: Reflections on the Twenty Years Since Oberhausen* (1984), a scholarly account of the New German Cinema and its historical-economic contexts.

Italian filmmaking is the subject of Pierre Leprohon, *The Italian Cinema* (1972; originally published in French, 1966); James Hay, *Popular Film Culture in Fascist Italy: The Passing of the Rex* (1987); Mira Liehm, *Passion and Defiance: Film in Italy from 1942 to the Present* (1984), an informative though sometimes eccentric critical study; Roy Armes, *Patterns of Realism* (1971, reprinted 1986), a standard study of the Neorealist cinema; and Peter Bondanella, *Italian Cinema: From Neorealism to the Present* (1983), a definitive scholarly analysis.

Films from the Soviet Union and eastern European countries are the subject of Jay

Leyda, *Kino: A History of the Russian and Soviet Film*, 3rd ed. (1983), a broad, authoritative study of developments beginning with tsarist times; Mira Liehm and Antonín J. Liehm, *The Most Important Art: Eastern European Film After 1945* (1977), a survey of Soviet, Polish, Czechoslovak, Hungarian, Yugoslav, East German, Romanian, and Bulgarian cinema, illustrated with many rare stills; Ronald Holloway, *The Bulgarian Cinema* (1986), a well-illustrated study; Peter Hames, *The Czechoslovak New Wave* (1985); Graham Petrie, *History Must Answer to Man: The Contemporary Hungarian Cinema* (1978); and Daniel J. Goulding, *Liberated Cinema: The Yugoslav Experience* (1985), a critical history of the postwar period.

For other European countries, see Peter Cowie, *Swedish Cinema* (1966), and *Swedish Cinema from Ingeborg Holm to Fanny and Alexander* (1985); and Peter Besas, *Behind the Spanish Lens: Spanish Cinema Under Fascism and Democracy* (1985).

For a survey of Australian movies, see Graham Shirley and Brian Adams, *Australian Cinema, the First Eighty Years* (1983), a standard scholarly history covering developments to 1975; and Brian McFarlane, *Australian Cinema 1970–1985* (1987), a valuable account of Australia's unprecedented film explosion.

Filmmaking in Asian and African countries is discussed in Noël Burch, *To the Distant Observer: Form and Meaning in the Japanese Cinema*, rev. and ed. by Annette Michelson (1979), a classical study of the film form and its misinterpretations in the West; Tadao Sato, *Currents in Japanese Cinema*, trans. from Japanese (1982), original essays with a filmography to 1981; Audie Bock, *Japanese Film Directors* (1978, reprinted 1985), a scrupulously researched critical study of 10 directors spanning the history of the industry; Thomas Weisser and Yuko Mihara Weisser, *Japanese Cinema: The Essential Handbook*, 4th rev. ed. (1998); Joseph L. Anderson and Donald Richie, *The Japanese Film: Art and Industry*, expanded ed. (1982); Jay Leyda, *Dianying: An Account of Films and the Film Audience in China* (1972); Erik Barnouw and S. Krishnaswamy, *Indian Film*, 2nd ed. (1980), an authoritative study; T.M. Ramachandran (ed.), *70 Years of Indian Cinema, 1913–1983* (1985), a well-illustrated, extended history; Roy Armes, *Third World Film Making and the West* (1987), a historical overview that also includes discussions of Latin American cinema; and Ashish Rajadhyaksha and Paul Willemen, *Encyclopedia of Indian Cinema*, new rev. ed. (1999).

Book-length works on Latin America, Cuba, and Mexico include Jorge A. Schnitman, *Film*

Industries in Latin America: Dependency and Development (1984), an economic analysis from the silent era through the 1980s; Randal Johnson and Robert Stam (eds.), *Brazilian Cinema* (1982), a definitive English-language history; Michael Chanan, *The Cuban Image: Cinema and Cultural Politics in Cuba* (1985); Carl J. Mora, *Mexican Cinema: Reflections of a Society, 1896–1980* (1982), a scholarly critical history; and Chon A. Noriega (ed.), *Visible Nations: Latin American Cinema and Video* (2000).

The cinema of the United States is the subject of Robert Sklar, *Movie-Made America: A Social History of American Movies* (1975); Lewis Jacobs, *The Rise of the American Film, a Critical History*, expanded ed. (1968, reissued 1974), a detailed study with emphasis on trends and audience preference; David Bordwell, Kristin Thompson, and Janet Staiger, *The Classical Hollywood Cinema: Film Style & Mode of Production to 1960* (1985); Douglas Gomery, *The Hollywood Studio System* (1985); Andrew Sarris, *The American Cinema: Directors and Directions*, 1929–1968 (1968, reprinted 1985), a classic definition of the auteur theory and its critical application to American films and filmmakers; and Tino Balio (ed.), *The American Film Industry*, rev. ed. (1985), an anthology of historical scholarship and primary documents from the origins to the 1980s.

GENRE STUDIES

Thomas Schatz, *Hollywood Genres: Formulas, Filmmaking, and the Studio System* (1981), examines prevalent styles and forms. Nonfiction films are discussed in Richard Meran Barsam, *Nonfiction Film: A Critical History* (1973), which focuses on British and American documentaries; Richard Meran Barsam (ed.), *Nonfiction Film: Theory and Criticism* (1976); and Erik Barnouw, *Documentary: A History of the Non-Fiction Film*, rev. ed. (1983). War themes are explored in Craig W. Campbell, *Reel America and World War I: A Comprehensive Filmography and History of Motion Pictures in the United States, 1914–1920* (1985); and Jeanine Basinger, *The World War II Combat Film: Anatomy of a Genre* (1986).

Studies of the western, crime movies, and film noir include William K. Everson, *The Hollywood Western: 90 Years of Cowboys and Indians, Train Robbers, Sheriffs and Gunslingers, and Assorted Heroes and Desperados* (1992, rev. ed. of *A Pictorial History of the Western Film*, 1969); Jim Kitses, *Horizons West: Anthony Mann, Budd Boetticher, Sam Peckinpah: Studies of Authorship Within the Western* (1969); Jon Tuska, *The Filming of the West* (1976); Lawrence Alloway, *Violent America: The Movies, 1946–1964* (1971); Carlos Clarens, *Crime Movies:*

From Griffith to The Godfather and Beyond (1980), a historical cross-genre survey; Alain Silver and Elizabeth Ward (eds.), *Film Noir: An Encyclopedic Reference to the American Style*, 3rd ed. (1993), a critical reference work; Foster Hirsch, *The Dark Side of the Screen: Film Noir* (1981, reprinted 1983), an in-depth study; and Jon Tuska, *Dark Cinema: American Film Noir in Cultural Perspective* (1984). Experimental cinema is the subject of Sheldon Renan, *An Introduction to the American Underground Film* (1967). The social-issue movie is explored in Peter Roffman and Jim Purdy, *The Hollywood Social Problem Film: Madness, Despair, and Politics from the Depression to the Fifties* (1981). For feminist studies of Hollywood films, see Mary Ann Doane, *The Desire to Desire: The Woman's Film of the 1940s* (1987); and E. Ann Kaplan, *Women and Film: Both Sides of the Camera* (1983), which also covers independent films.

Two surveys of specific genres are Kalton C. Lahue, *Continued Next Week: A History of the Moving Picture Serial* (1964), and *World of Laughter: The Motion Picture Comedy Short, 1910–1930* (1966, reprinted 1972). Other works on comedy include Walter Kerr, *The Silent Clowns* (1975); Gerald Mast, *The Comic Mind: Comedy and the Movies*, 2nd ed. (1979), a thematic study of silent and sound comedies and the relationship between intellectual content and comic form; and Andrew Horton (ed.), *Comedy/Cinema/Theory* (1991).

Musicals are discussed in John Kobal, *A History of Movie Musicals: Gotta Sing, Gotta Dance*, rev. ed. (1983), an extremely well-represented international survey; Ted Sennett, *Hollywood Musicals* (1981, reprinted 1985); Jane Feuer, *The Hollywood Musical* (1982); Rick Altman, *The American Film Musical* (1987, reissued 1989), a definitive study of the structure of the genre; and Colin Larkin, *The Virgin Encyclopedia of Stage and Film Musicals* (1999).

For an overview of animated films, see Leonard Maltin, *Of Mice and Magic: A History of American Animated Cartoons* (1980); Donald Crafton, *Before Mickey: The Animated Film, 1898–1928* (1982), a scholarly discussion of pre-Disney works; and Christopher Finch, *The Art of Walt Disney: From Mickey Mouse to the Magic Kingdoms* (1973, reprinted 1983), a richly illustrated study.

INDEX

D

E

F

T

Z